Our Simmering Planet

WHAT TO DO ABOUT GLOBAL WARMING?

JOYEETA GUPTA

A BRAVE NEW SERIES

GLOBAL ISSUES IN A CHANGING WORLD

This new series of short, accessible think-pieces deals with leading global issues of relevance to humanity today. Intended for the enquiring reader and social activists in the North and the South, as well as students, the books explain what is at stake and question conventional ideas and policies. Drawn from many different parts of the world, the series' authors pay particular attention to the needs and interests of ordinary people, whether living in the rich industrial or the developing countries. They all share a common objective – to help stimulate new thinking and social action in the opening years of the new century.

Global Issues in a Changing World is a joint initiative by Zed Books in collaboration with a number of partner publishers and non-governmental organizations around the world. By working together, we intend to maximize the relevance and availability of the books published in the series.

PARTICIPATING NGOs

Both ENDS, Amsterdam
Catholic Institute for International Relations, London
Corner House, Sturminster Newton
Council on International and Public Affairs, New York
Dag Hammarskjöld Foundation, Uppsala
Development GAP, Washington DC
Focus on the Global South, Bangkok
Inter Pares, Ottawa
Public Interest Research Centre, Delhi
Third World Network, Penang
Third World Network–Africa, Accra
World Development Movement, London

About the Author

JOYEETA GUPTA studied economics at Delhi University (India), law at Gujarat University (India) and Harvard Law School (USA), and acquired her doctorate from the Vrije Universiteit in Amsterdam (Netherlands). She has worked for non-governmental organisations in India (Consumer Education and Research Centre, Ahmedabad), the USA (Ralph Nader's Centre for the Study of Responsive Law in Washington) and the Netherlands (the International Organisation of Consumers' Unions). Since 1991 she has worked mostly on climate change, at the Netherlands' Ministry of Housing, Spatial Planning and the Environment, and since 1993 at the Institute for Environmental Studies, Amsterdam. She has published extensively on the subject of climate change.

A GLOBAL ISSUES TITLE

OUR SIMMERING PLANET

What to do about global warming?

JOYEETA GUPTA

ZED BOOKS
London & New York

UNIVERSITY PRESS LTD
Dhaka

WHITE LOTUS CO. LTD
Bangkok

FERNWOOD PUBLISHING LTD
Halifax, Nova Scotia

DAVID PHILIP
Cape Town

BOOKS FOR CHANGE
Bangalore

Our Simmering Planet
was first published in 2001 by

In Bangladesh: The University Press Ltd, Red Crescent Building,
114, Motijheel C/A, PO Box 2611, Dhaka 1000

In Burma, Cambodia, Laos, Thailand and Vietnam:
White Lotus Co. Ltd, GPO Box 1141, Bangkok 10501, Thailand

In Canada: Fernwood Publishing Ltd, PO Box 9409, Station A,
Halifax, Nova Scotia, Canada B3K 5S3

In India: Books for Change, SKIP House,
25/1 Museum Road, Bangalore 560025

In Southern Africa: David Philip Publishers (Pty Ltd),
208 Werdmuller Centre, Claremont 7735, South Africa

In the rest of the world:
Zed Books Ltd, 7 Cynthia Street, London N1 9JF UK and
Room 400, 175 Fifth Avenue, New York, NY 10010, USA

Distributed in the USA exclusively by Palgrave, a division of
St Martin's Press, LLC, 175 Fifth Avenue, New York, NY 10010

Cover designed by Andrew Corbett
Designed and typeset in Monotype Bembo by Illuminati, Grosmont
Printed and bound in the United Kingdom by Cox & Wyman, Reading

A catalogue record for this book is available from the British Library

US CIP data is available from the Library of Congress

Canadian CIP data is available from the National Library of Canada

ISBN 1 55266 067 2 Pb. (Canada)

ISBN 0 86486 513 9 Pb. (Southern Africa)

ISBN 1 84277 078 0 Hb. (Zed Books)

ISBN 1 84277 079 9 Pb. (Zed Books)

Contents

List of Tables, Figures and Boxes

ACKNOWLEDGEMENTS

This book is based on years of on-going research on climate change. Most of the work written till now has been academic in nature and accessible mostly to readers in the North. I have wanted to write a serious book that is more accessible to the general public, especially in the developing world.

Although the book is meant to be comprehensible to the general public, I have tried not to sacrifice detail and fact. I am much indebted to the following people who have inspired me over the years in relation to the need to focus on North–South issues: Professor Manubhai Shah, who introduced me to the need for consumer protection; Ralph Nader, for his inspiring speeches and books; Professor Pier Vellinga, for his support over the last ten years; members of the Climate Change Knowledge Network; and many others.

In relation to this particular book, I would like to thank Robert Molteno and Michael Pallis of Zed for commenting on the manuscript. In particular, I would like to thank Hans van der Hoeven for his constant support and encouragement over the years and for his advice on the manuscript. Many thanks to Eileen Harloff, a dear friend, who helped with the text.

ABBREVIATIONS

AIJ	activities implemented jointly
AOSIS	Alliance of Small Island States
ASEAN	Association of South-East Asian Nations
CAN	Climate Action Network
CANSEA	Climate Action Network South-East Asia
CDF	Clean Development Fund
CDM	Clean Development Mechanism
CIT	country in transition to a market economy
CNA	Climate Network Africa
CNE	Climate Network Europe
COP	Conference of the Parties
CSD	Commission for Sustainable Development
CSE	Centre for Science and Environment (New Delhi)
CTBT	Comprehensive Test Ban Treaty
DC	developing country
ECOWAS	Economic Community of West African States
EPA	Environmental Protection Agency
FCCC	United Nations Framework Convention on Climate Change
G8	Group of 8 (the G7 countries and the Russian Federation)
G77	Group of 77 (comprises 133 members, of which 130 are active)

GATT	General Agreement on Tariffs and Trade
GDP	Gross Domestic Product
GEF	Global Environment Facility
GHG	greenhouse gas
GWP	Global Warming Potential
HIDC	High-Income Developing Country
IBRD	International Bank for Reconstruction and Development
IC	industrialised country
ICJ	International Court of Justice
ICLEI	International Council for Local Environmental Initiatives
IGADD	Intergovernmental Authority on Drought and Development
IMF	International Monetary Fund
INC	Intergovernmental Negotiating Committee (on the FCCC)
IPCC	Intergovernmental Panel on Climate Change
IPCC–SAR	IPCC–Second Assessment Report
IPR	intellectual property rights
ITTO	International Tropical Timber Organisation
JI	joint implementation
JICA	Japan International Co-operation Agency
JUSSCANNZ	Japan, US, Switzerland, Canada, Australia, Norway and New Zealand
KPFCCC	Kyoto Protocol to the FCCC
LBO	legally binding objectives
LBRO	legally binding reduction objectives
LBSO	legally binding stabilisation objectives
LDC	less developed country
MIDC	middle-income developing country
NAM	Non-Aligned Movement
NGO	Non-Governmental Organisation
NIEO	New International Economic Order
NIMBY	not in my back yard
OAU	Organisation of African Unity

ODA	official development assistance
OECD	Organisation for Economic Co-operation and Development
OPEC	Organisation of Petroleum Exporting Countries
PPP	purchasing power parity
SAARC	South Asia Association for Regional Cooperation
SADC	Southern African Development Community
SAP	structural adjustment programme
SIDC	small island developing country
SWCC	Second World Climate Conference
TEP	tradeable emission permits
TERI	Tata Energy Research Institute (New Delhi)
TNC	transnational corporation
UN	United Nations
UNCED	United Nations Conference on Environment and Development
UNCTAD	United Nations Conference on Trade and Development
UNDP	United Nations Development Programme
UNEP	United Nations Environment Programme
UNGA	United Nations General Assembly
WBCSD	World Business Council for Sustainable Development
WCED	World Commission on Environment and Development
WRI	World Resources Institute (Washington DC)
WTO	World Trade Organisation

CHEMICAL NAMES

CO_2	carbon dioxide
CFC	chlorofluorocarbons
CH_4	methane
PFCs	perfluorocarbons
NMHC	non-methane hydrocarbons
N_2O	nitrous oxide
SF_6	sulphur hexafluoride

CHAPTER I

WEATHERING THE WEATHER

There is an old fable about a frog in a pan of water. If you put a frog in a pan of boiling water, it will jump out. If you put the frog in a pan of cold water which is then slowly put to cook, it may get accustomed to the rising temperatures and gradually lose its reactive functions and die. I have no clue as to the origin of this fable, but the message is unmistakable and it is ominous.

We live in a simmering planet, in two senses. Temperatures are alleged to be gradually rising and there is increasing evidence of global warming. Climatic variations and extreme weather conditions are being experienced worldwide. The fact that modern media immediately communicate events globally tends to have a magnifying effect in respect of these events. Meanwhile, people all over the world face weather-related challenges.

At the same time, tensions that have been ebbing and flowing between countries in the last century have reached a point where, though it appears everyone is ready to collaborate, a cauldron of discontent is ready to bubble over. This is visible in the statement of the very first summit of the group of developing countries – the G77 – which took place in 2000 (see Box 12), a statement that did not get much attention in the western world. While there have been attempts to gloss over the discontent and to point to the areas of agreement reached between North and South, the (lack of) new global leadership may engender more tensions between countries.

Against this background, this book examines the evidence of climate change, and asks whether the world is indeed simmering enough to take action.

LOCAL WEATHER CALAMITIES OCCURRING GLOBALLY

During the last decade there have been more frequent reports of extreme weather. In 1990, floods in eastern Australia left building foundations unstable, people homeless, 150,000 livestock lost and transport and business damaged. In the same year there was severe rainfall in Burma, Bangladesh and India. Forest fires destroyed 600,000 hectares of forest in Mongolia. There were summer fires in France and Italy and severe drought along the Nile, and in Ethiopia, Japan, Peru, Sudan, Turkey, Tuvalu and the United Kingdom. There were heat waves in England and Wales, hurricanes in the eastern Pacific, typhoons in China, Japan and the Philippines, blizzards in the Alps and winter chill in California. In 1991, there were hot spells or drought in regions ranging from Alaska, Oregon and California to northern Argentina, Uruguay, Paraguay, southern Brazil and Indonesia. There was flooding on the Yangtse, typhoons in Japan and cyclones in Bangladesh and the Pacific. A year later there were droughts in parts of America, Africa and Asia, hurricanes in the Pacific, tornadoes in the US and melting glaciers in the Swiss Alps. A World Meteorological Organisation bulletin in 1993 reported that weather-related events killed more than 41,000 people in 68 countries between 1987 and 1992, and caused the loss of more than US$35 billion in 1992 alone. An insurance company, Munich Re, concluded that there were 100 more natural disasters in 1992 than in previous years and that the losses had reached a value of US$27.1 billion, an increase of 87 per cent on the previous year (Greenpeace 1994: 96). In 1993 there were reports of droughts in Alaska, eastern Australia, Greece, Spain and the UK; flooding in Belgium, France, Germany, Italy, the Netherlands and Switzerland; typhoons in Japan, and tornadoes in the US mid-west.

In the five years that followed, there were continuing reports of extreme weather events all over the globe. The year 2000 saw unusual flooding in Australia and Britain in addition to other weather calamities the world over. Kluger and Lemonick (2001) report that Mount Kilimanjaro has lost 75 per cent of its ice cap since 1912, and it may melt completely in 15 years. Of the six glaciers in Venezuela, only two remain. The Glacier National Park in Montana in the US is expected to lose its ice cover by 2070. Across the US there were extremely hot spells in 2000, and in May of that year it was reported that some 2,500 people died in India in a heat wave, the worst in fifty years. There was flooding in Australia, and in Ohio floods led to 30 deaths and the loss of US$500 million in property damage. In 1999 and in 2001 floods left the state of Orissa in India devastated. Slow-melting ice blocks in the rising Lena river in Russia have been a recent source of much disruption in the lives of the people along its banks. There are reports practically every week in 2001 of weather-related events worldwide.

Communications are shrinking the world. Flooding in Australia in late 2000, or a cyclone in Orissa, is world news. Do we hear so much about all these climatic disasters because of the role of the international media in the last decade, or is there a definite trend in the number of weather calamities, and do these indicate increasing instability in the global climate? These are questions that the second chapter of this book seeks to answer.

THE CAULDRON OF DISCONTENT

The global community (is there one?) has seen much progress and much dissension over the last century. Does a book on climate change need to look at the history of global relations? I think so, not just because of the long history of the climate-change problem, but also because, from the perspective of many in the South, the reaction of the developed countries is consistent with their reactions to earlier situations of a comparable nature. If people in the South have learnt anything from history, it is that that the rich and developed would like to keep their wealth and can shape international discussions to ensure that they succeed in doing so. This may sound hysterical to some, and nonsensical to others. But the perception remains. Is it justified? I would invite the readers of this book to judge the facts for themselves.

Let us undertake a brief journey through the second half of the last century from the perspective of North–South relations. With the establishment of the Bretton Woods institutions – the International Monetary Fund (IMF) and the International Bank for Reconstruction and Development (IBRD) – in 1944, reconstruction and development of the developing countries was given prominence. Although peace and development have been on the UN's agenda since 1945, developmental issues have been given only ineffective lip-service (Roberts and Kingsbury 1993).

With the end of colonialism, three different trends were visible in the developing countries: the continuation of colonial politics and practices by newly established domestic regimes, the pursuit of change, and an unhappy mixture of the two (cf. Salah 1993: 54–5; Kothari 1993: 86; Dadzie 1993). It was in this period that the concept of development planning was exported to developing countries, and they adopted approaches that were to help them to reach development. In the second phase (1963–82), developing countries argued in favour of a fair framework of international economic relations to improve their chances of development. At the same time, the IMF and the World Bank were seen as imposing new conditions on them. The difficulty experienced by the developing countries in articulating and supporting their perspectives on various international issues led them to establish the Group of 77 (G77) within the framework of the United Nations (see pp. 102–5). In the 1970s the developing countries fought for a new international economic order (NIEO). Their optimism was short-lived: although three instruments were adopted – the Declaration on the New International Economic Order, a Programme of Action, and a Charter of Economic Rights and Duties of States – not much was ever implemented.

Since the 1940s the gap between the average developing country and the average developed country has been increasing. Per capita incomes in the developed and developing countries will probably continue to diverge well into the new century (Pritchett 1996; UNDP 1996; UNEP 2000). Furthermore, there has been a decrease in official development assistance (ODA) over the years. The G7 countries spent only 0.19 per cent of their collective GNP on ODA in 1997, while other OECD countries provided 0.45 per cent as compared to their stated commitment of 0.7 per cent (Agenda 21 1992: paras 33.16–18). ODA fell from US$54.4 billion in 1996 to US$47.6 billion in 1997. Whereas the environmental assistance funds were meant to be 'new and additional', evidence suggests that it is existing ODA funds that are now being diverted to environmental issues (or just being reduced). The diversion of ODA resources from local environmental priorities to global environmental priorities is in practice a further constraint on the development prospects of the developing countries.

The concerns of these two groups of countries, while focused on economic growth, diverge in terms of actual policy priorities. This is especially evident in international forums where negotiations on a number of economic, trade-related and environmental issues tend to take the form of North–South debate. In the view of the developing countries, whenever they were able to articulate their views effectively in a particular UN forum, the issue was then moved to an alternative forum. For example, the intellectual property rights discussion moved from the World Intellectual Property Rights Organisation through the General Agreement on Tariffs and Trade (GATT) to the World Trade Organisation (WTO). UN bodies such as the United Nations Environment Programme (UNEP), the United Nations Conference on Trade and Development (UNCTAD) and Habitat, which had often supported the developing countries, were marginalised until the structures became more friendly to the North (Gosovic 1992). Even though the world was ostensibly in favour of free trade, import tariffs in the OECD countries prevented developing countries from marketing the products in which they had a competitive advantage (Nath 1993). Prices of raw materials kept falling because of the export regime, and international pricing practices led to resource and labour exploitation in the South. Meanwhile the debt problem in the South had reached overwhelming proportions and the indebted countries were unable to cope (George 1992). The solution adopted was not to reduce tariff barriers in the West and to raise the prices of raw materials to reflect the real ecological cost of using up finite natural resources, but to impose structural adjustment programmes (SAPs) on southern countries, leading to even more severe crises, with education and health receiving lower priorities than ever before. Excitement in the South at the prospect of developing and becoming rich like the developed countries gave way to the realisation that this so-called 'graduation' would remain for many an impossible dream. Dogged by debt and civil crises, the 1980s were seen as the lost decade for development.

The discussion between the North and the South during the 1992 United Nations Conference on Environment and Development (UNCED) was a conflict over how the two goals should be integrated. In the 1990s the developing countries were, on the one hand, facing the complicated implications of the global environmental crisis while, on the other hand, dealing with the tentacles of globalisation. Globalisation was and is expected to lead to one united world through the expansion of world trade, media coverage and the world wide web. However, these very trends can lead to the further marginalisation of the poorer sections of the South. This may happen through distorted media coverage, increased liberalisation on the one hand and 'closed' markets on the other, foreign debt, and disempowerment of those not connected to the web. According to the South Centre prices in commodity markets have been depressed, exports from developing countries have faced barriers, and international interest rates have been high (South Centre 1993: 4). Furthermore, the division between hard and soft currency is seen as another tool used by the developed countries to protect their advantages (Galtung 1993: 78). Amin identifies polarisation mechanisms that result from globalisation, including selective labour migration (the brain drain), control by the North of access to the natural resources of the South, and monopoly positions held by companies belonging to the North (Amin 1993: 133). While globalisation appears to lead to 'one world', the fear is that it will lead only to a worldwide community of elite people while the vast majority of the earth's population will live on the periphery.

One may even speculate that this elite might live in Bangalore in India and work for international computer companies, and that educational and professional qualifications will appear to be more important than nationality, but the essential features of the divide will remain. Pfaff, a columnist with the *International Herald Tribune*, explains that colonialism and globalisation might be eerily similar (Pfaff 2001). In both cases the motivation is to find markets, cheap raw materials and labour. The questions that remain are: can globalisation happen without exploitation; can it promote democratisation? Even colonialism apparently aimed at civilising the world, states Pfaff, citing the *Encyclopaedia Britannica*. The moral arguments behind colonialism in the 1920s and 1930s show similarity with the modern day arguments in favour of globalisation. In fact, modern day globalisation, like its predecessor, disrupts political and social structures, damages cultural infrastructure and tends to make small businesses and local companies bankrupt because of their inability to compete with modern multinationals.

At the same time, areas where the South had a competitive advantage are being redefined as domains of the North. The wealth of seeds and crops in the South is suddenly coming under the purview of the North via international pressure by giant corporations to grow genetically engineered crops that are likely to marginalise further the small farmer (De La Perrière and Seurat 2000). There is fear that southern seeds and plants are being patented in the North (WRI 1994: 123). Engineered free trade is seen as a mechanism to benefit transnational corporations at the cost of the small farmer and the millions of malnourished people (Madeley 2000). Liberalisation and privatisation of water markets may lead to further disempowerment of the 1.5 billion people that do not have access to clean water (Petrella 2001). Quick-fix solutions of development dispensed by the World Bank and its associates are still missing the point. People in the developing countries do not have access to basic resources, nor will their access increase overnight simply by guaranteeing multinationals access to domestic markets and protecting the interests of large companies. Development needs to be demystified (De Rivero 2001).

Apart from the gap in terms of financial resources and ideologies, governance patterns differ strongly between the developed and the developing countries. Institutions are built in totally different ways. Given weak institutions, corruption is rife in many developing countries, and many are in a state of constitutional crisis. Since they are continually trying to cope with domestic crises, these states have not been able to keep pace with developments on the international front. There are also some developing countries that are extremely rich. Chile, Israel, Saudi Arabia, Singapore, South Korea and Qatar, for example, have high per capita income levels, although they may share structural problems and cultural and geographical features with other developing countries. In the course of time, they may move out of the G77, but whatever movement there may be at the margin, this does not detract from the essential argument that there will be key features affecting the less powerful countries in the world.

The South consists of 3.5 billion people living in 150 countries in thousands of communities with divergent religions, languages, customs and resources. However, it also exists as a loosely united body defined by its geographical location, its shared structural and political short-comings, its use of soft currency and its common historical experiences. '[T]hey share a fundamental trait: they exist on the periphery of the developed countries of the North. Most of their people are poor; their economies are mostly weak and defenceless; they are generally powerless in the world arena' (South Centre 1993: 3).

ARE WE AT BOILING POINT?

The North–South divide is becoming increasingly evident in the area of climate-change negotiations. The North, defined as around 40 countries in the climate treaties (see Chapters 3 and 6), emitted 75 per cent of the annual carbon dioxide emissions in 1990. Its contribution to the carbon dioxide concentrations in the atmosphere stood at 79 per cent in 1990. This implies that its share of induced temperature increase is calculated at 88 per cent (note by Secretariat to AGBM 1997). While in the early 1990s the developing countries pointed out the extreme pollution caused by the North, in recent months it has been the Americans that have focused on the need for the developing countries to take action. This brings us to the climate-change issue and what it means for North–South relations. But before delving into the complexity to be discussed in considerable detail in the following chapters, it might be well to paint a simple picture of what is happening.

If a neighbourhood factory pollutes the nearby stream causing damage to the citizens, then in most countries in the world the factory would be held responsible for cleaning up the mess. This is based on the notion that those who cause harm must be held liable. It is sometimes referred to as the 'polluter pays principle'.

Climate change is caused principally by greenhouse gases (GHGs) being emitted in the energy and transport sector, and by land-use change (see Chapter 2). However, although the pollution can be attributed to certain types of activities and industries, countries have identified their interests with those industries undertaking such activities and they shy away from a discussion of the polluter pays principle and liability. A convenient argument is that the exact cause–effect relationship between the emissions and the impacts cannot be ascertained and that, in effect, all countries are polluters and hence all are responsible. A follow-up argument is that it is pointless to take action in developed countries if the developing countries then continue to pollute the atmosphere since this will render the impacts of such actions negligible.

The problem with climate change is that it concerns a relatively restricted resource (the so-called 'environment utilisation space') that has to be shared by people who are not exactly friendly to each other. People would thus like to develop rules for sharing that best meet their own needs. In the past, water in international rivers was shared between countries on the basis of 'prior appropriation'. This means that if a country has traditionally used more water, then it acquires a historical right to the water, and the other country automatically gets only what is left over. Today, a new version of this principle is emerging. Thus countries are arguing that if they have polluted the atmosphere more than others, and if there is only a limited space for polluting that atmosphere, then in effect they have a historical right to that level of pollution. Of course nobody spells this out quite so graphically. Nevertheless, the argument is implicit in the discussion regarding the flexibility mechanisms that have been developed in the climate change convention (see Chapter 4).

And so although in the initial enthusiasm of dealing with a new problem the developed countries promised to lead the South into a GHG-free world, this initiative has backfired, with the United States reneging on its leadership role and demanding action from developing countries as a precondition for accepting legally binding commitments. The rest of the developed countries do not really wish to ratify the agreement until and unless the US does so, and the developing countries do not wish to pick up the baton. Nevertheless, the negotiation dynamics have reached such a point that it appears that the rest of the world is willing to go ahead without US support.

The irony of the problem is that although the major polluters thus far may be in the developed countries of the North, they are in a better position – or at least so they think – to be able to cope with the impacts of climate change. If there is heat stress, one can sit in an air-conditioned car or office; if there is a problem with the temperature, one can just adjust heating and water systems; if the sea level threatens to rise, one can build additional dikes, dams and dunes. There is a feeling that there may not be quite that much to lose. This feeling is especially echoed in the US Republican Party and their sponsors in industry. While Europe espouses the rhetoric of responsibility for taking action, it is sometimes convenient to hide behind the US position. The same is probably true for some larger developing countries who would prefer to ignore the implications of the problem rather than look it in the eye. Meanwhile, small island nations, arid and semi-arid African countries, and coastal areas in the developing world are calling for action.

The discussions are beset with accusations of free-riding. A free-rider is one who, despite his own inaction, benefits from the actions of others. Some developed countries accuse the developing countries of shirking their responsibilities in relation to climate change and wanting to take a free ride on the action to be taken by the North. The South argues that it is precisely the North that has taken a free ride on the South, since it has been the main polluter thus far, and that it is using the free-rider argument to force environmental constraints on the developmental agenda of the South. This leads experts from the developing world to insist that 'the North with its indisputable power should not make the environmental issue a new instrument of domination over the South' (Khor 2001: 125).

WHERE TO?

It seems increasingly clear that there are a number of climatic disasters taking place around the globe, and these appear to be increasing in intensity. We seem to be living on a simmering planet. Whether this is a trend out of the ordinary still remains to be determined. However, with increasing populations living in coastal and vulnerable areas, more people seem to be affected by these calamities than ever before. If indeed these extreme calamities are the result of human activity, we are playing with fire. If they are the result of the vagaries of nature, we still have to prepare ourselves to cope with them and to withstand the effects. And if this is the mysterious hand of God, only a latter-day Noah and his entourage are likely to survive.

Martin Khor argues in his book *Rethinking Globalisation* that developing countries need to be careful about welcoming globalisation and liberalisation, and should adopt a selective approach in order to protect small producers and benefit customers (Khor 2001). At the same time, given the nature of the battles the developing countries have been losing in the international environmental arena, it is perhaps time for them to take stock of the situation and see what they can do to help themselves.

CHAPTER 2

CLIMATE INSTABILITY AND GLOBAL WARMING: THE EVIDENCE

> The devil can cite Scripture for his purpose.
> Shakespeare, *The Merchant of Venice*

If the scriptures can be misquoted by the devil, why should relatively mundane documents like the scientific reports on climate change not be quoted to suit the purpose of the citer? Climate change, alas, appears to be a problem in the eye of the beholder.

The last chapter referred to the extreme weather events that have been experienced the world over. Of course these events do not pass unnoticed in the scientific world. Are they caused by climate change?

Although scientific work has been undertaken since the early nineteenth century, such work increased rapidly in the second half of the twentieth century. In 1827 Fourier postulated the theory that humans could affect the climate. In 1896 Arrhenius tried to show the relationship between fossil-fuel burning and warming. And finally, in 1979, the first World Climate Conference was held. At this Conference the available evidence was discussed: 'the Conference finds that it is now urgently necessary for the nations of the world … to foresee and to prevent potential man-made changes in climate that might be adverse to the well-being of humanity'.

A decade later, an Advisory Group on the Greenhouse Effect was established. It laid the groundwork for the establishment of the Intergovernmental Panel on Climate Change (IPCC) by the World Meteorological Organisation and the United Nations Environment

Programme. IPCC has a bureau and a secretariat. The bureau consists of the Chairman, five Vice-Chairmen, Co-Chairmen and the chairs of the Working Groups. The bureau is expected to have balanced geographical representation and include experts with relevant scientific and technical qualifications. The secretariat is based in Geneva. There are three Working Groups, on Science (the scientific aspects of the climate-change system), Impact and Adaptation (the vulnerability of human and natural systems to climate change and options for adaptation), and Mitigation (options for limiting greenhouse gases and mitigating climate change). There is also a Task Force on National Greenhouse Gas Inventories. Each Working Group and the Task Force has a Technical Support Unit in the UK, USA, Netherlands and Japan respectively. If requested, the IPCC may initiate special reports on specific subjects, but it does not carry out its own research; it merely assesses the existing peer-reviewed and published research work. Most of this research is carried out within the framework of the World Climate Research Programme, the International Geosphere–Biosphere Programme, the International Human Dimensions of Global Environmental Change and the existing monitoring work that is carried out within the framework of the World Weather Watch, the Global Atmospheric Watch, the Global Climate Observing System, the Global Terrestrial Observing System and the Global Ocean Observing System. In 1990 the IPCC came out with its first assessment reports on climate change; the second set was published in 1995; and the third is expected in 2001.

What is Climate Change?

The climate over a period of time is defined by IPCC as the 'averages of appropriate components of the weather over that period, together with the statistical variations of those components' (Houghton *et al.* 1990: xxxv). The earth's climatic system is the result of complex interrelationships between processes in the atmosphere, geosphere, ocean, ice (cryosphere) and biosphere, and is driven by energy from the sun. Solar radiation enters the earth's atmosphere as short-wave radiation and is partly absorbed by the land and partly reflected back into space. The energy absorbed by the earth must be balanced by outgoing long-wave infra-red terrestrial radiation. This radiation can be partially absorbed by certain gases and then re-emitted into space. These gases, such as carbon dioxide, methane and nitrogen oxide, are called *greenhouse gases* (GHGs) and their existence in the earth's atmosphere leads to the *greenhouse effect*. Some of these emissions are natural and some are *anthropogenic* (human induced). The increase in the concentration of greenhouse gases leads to the *enhanced* greenhouse effect, which is the critical issue in the climate change problem.

The most important greenhouse gases are the three mentioned above, with carbon dioxide playing the most significant role. Other greenhouse gases include the halocarbons such as chlorofluorocarbons (CFCs: $CFCl_3$, CF_2Cl_2, etc.), their substitute compounds (CHF_2Cl, CF_3CH_2F, etc.) and synthetic compounds such as perfluorocarbons (PFCs), sulphur hexafluoride (SF_6), water vapour and ozone. Water vapour has a very large greenhouse effect, but its concentration in the troposphere (the lowest atmospheric level) is determined by the climate system itself. Ozone is a greenhouse gas that accumulates in the troposphere either through transport from the stratospheric ozone layer, or photo-oxidation of carbon monoxide, methane and non-methane hydrocarbons (NMHC) in the presence of nitrogen oxides. The latter are referred to as the precursors of tropospheric ozone.

These gases have different *lifetimes* in the atmosphere. Water vapour lasts for about a week, methane and HCFC22 for about a decade, CFC11 for 50 years, nitrous oxide for more than 120 years and carbon dioxide anything between 50 and 200 years. This means that even if emissions of these gases are reduced, their concentration is not affected immediately. To stabilise or reduce atmospheric concentrations, it is therefore essential to reduce emissions drastically. It is important here to specify that although individual molecules of carbon dioxide may be absorbed within a few years in oceans and biomass, the lifetime refers to the time it takes for the atmospheric CO_2 level to adjust to a new equilibrium if the sources or sinks change (see pp. 20–2).

Each gas has a different potential to warm the atmosphere. This *global warming potential* (GWP) is measured in comparison to the *radiative forcing* of carbon dioxide, which is denoted as 1. This allows for calculating the time-integrated warming effect from the release of 1 kg of a greenhouse gas relative to that of carbon dioxide. Thus, if the GWP of carbon dioxide is 1 for a twenty-year period, that of methane is 63, of nitrous oxide 270, and of CFC11 4,500. Over a 100-year period, if the GWP of carbon dioxide is 1, that of methane is 21, of nitrous oxide 290, and CFC11 3,500. This means that the gases can be measured in terms of *carbon dioxide equivalence*. These values can change over time as the composition of the atmosphere changes (Houghton *et al.* 1990). This concept allows for comparison between the gases.

The climate is not, however, a simple linear system. It is affected by the variability in solar radiation received because of changes in the earth's orbital patterns or by changes in the total solar irradiance. At the same time, anthropogenic sulphur emissions lead to the formation of aerosols which influence the radiative properties of clouds and can have a cooling effect. The climate is also affected by the planetary *albedo*. Part of the incoming radiation is reflected out by the surface of the earth and by the atmosphere. This reflectance varies with the object and with the wave-length of the radiation. The albedo of an object is the reflectance averaged out over all wave-lengths (Jansen 1999: 36). Clouds are made of water vapour and thus absorb outgoing radiation. But clouds also reflect part of the incoming radiation. Greenhouse gas emissions increase the potential to warm the earth's atmosphere. However, each gas is cycled between the various sources and sinks and these cycles are affected by different forces. Furthermore, each gas has a direct and an indirect effect on warming. The indirect effects depend on the chemical processes that influence the concentration of the gas in the atmosphere. There are also many positive and negative feedback effects that influence the climate. For example, as the earth warms, there is more evaporation leading to increased water vapour which leads to further warming. This is a positive feedback effect.

LABORATORY MODELS AND PREDICTIONS

The fact is that the global average surface temperature increased in the twentieth century by 0.6 ($\pm$ 0.2) degrees Centigrade. It is 90-99 per cent likely that the 1990s were the warmest decade, and that 1998 was the hottest year since 1861. On the basis of data for the northern hemisphere, the recent IPCC report concludes that the increase in temperature in the twentieth century is likely to have been the greatest in the last 1000 years. Snow cover has decreased by 10 per cent since the 1960s. The average sea level has risen by 0.1–0.2 metres during the twentieth century. Precipitation has increased by 0.5–1 per cent per decade in the twentieth century in the mid and high latitudes of the northern hemisphere, and by 0.2–0.3 per cent per decade in tropical land areas. But the rainfall has decreased by about 0.3 per cent per decade in the sub-tropical regions of the northern hemisphere. The frequency and intensity of droughts have increased in Asia and Africa. There have been more frequent and more persistent warm episodes of the El Niño–Southern Oscillation phenomenon which affects the regional climate (IPCC-I 2001). The IPCC report thus concludes that there are measurable changes in the atmosphere.

Is this caused by human activity? The report states that the atmospheric concentration of CO_2 has increased by 31 per cent since 1750, a rate that has probably not been experienced in the last 20 million years. About 75 per cent of anthropogenic emissions come from fossil-fuel burning, and the rest is from land-use change and deforestation. Methane concentrations have increased by 151 per cent since 1750, and this degree of concentration has not been experienced in the last 420,000 years. About half of the emissions are from anthropogenic sources (which include wet rice cultivation, the rumination of animals, and the use of fossil fuels). Nitrous oxide concentrations have increased by 17 per cent since 1750, of which about one third is anthropogenic. Although halocarbons have decreased since 1995, their substitutes are increasing. Tropospheric ozone concentrations have increased by 36 per cent since 1750 because of the emissions of ozone-forming gases (precursors).

How do these gases influence climate? Although a lot is known about the radiative forcing of these gases, less is known about the impacts of organic and black carbon from fossil-fuel burning, biomass burning and mineral dust, or the indirect effects of aerosols and

TABLE 1   The increasing concentration of key greenhouse gases in the atmosphere

Gas	Increase in concentration since 1750	Comment
CO_2	31%	Not exceeded in last 420,000 years at least
CH_4	151%	Not exceeded in last 420,000 years
N_2O	17%	Not exceeded during last 10,000 years at least

Source: derived from IPCC-I 2001.

solar warming. Further there are some cooling effects from the depletion of the stratospheric ozone layer, the accumulation of sulphates and aerosols, and biomass burning, which are less understood. However, the depletion of the ozone layer is being addressed and the cooling effects will thus be temporary. The report concludes: 'In the light of new evidence and taking into account the remaining uncertainties, most of the observed warming over the last 50 years is likely (66–90 per cent) to have been due to the increase in greenhouse gas concentrations. Furthermore, it is very likely (90–99 per cent) that the 20th century warming has contributed significantly to the observed sea level rise, through thermal expansion of sea water and widespread loss of land ice' (IPCC-I 2001: 10).

And if indeed these gases are accumulating, how will they influence the climate in the future? The information regarding emission trajectories is fed into a number of models to generate data about the future. These models conclude that the global average surface temperature is projected to increase by 1.4–5.8 degrees Centigrade over the period 1990–2100. Precipitation is likely (66–90 per cent) to increase in the northern mid to high latitudes, but will vary in the lower latitudes. There will be more uncertainty regarding the degree of precipitation every year. Regarding the possibility of extreme weather events, the report is more cautious and says that while higher maximum and minimum temperatures, more hot days and fewer cold days and more intense precipitation are very likely (90–99 per cent) on land masses everywhere, there is less certainty about the predictions of tropical cyclones and drought (partly because of lack of data). The global sea level is expected to rise by 0.09–0.88 metres between 1990 and 2100. It is also expected that the ocean thermohaline circulation (which transports warm water to the North Atlantic) could slow down and even stop beyond 2100; this could lead to drastic changes overall.

THE SIGNIFICANCE OF LABORATORY PREDICTIONS

The information provided by IPCC contains some facts and some speculation. The facts are in general not disputed as much as the speculation. The climatic system is very complicated, being affected by a number of inter-related causes. Compiling evidence calls for sophisticated data from a number of scientific sources and filling in the gaps in knowledge with some assumptions and theories. This compilation of data is part of a huge consensus enterprise between scientists and policy-makers worldwide. How convincing is it for those outside the system?

The sceptics argue that the information is so scant that trying to complete the picture makes for unreliable science. In particular they point out that the IPCC reports do not give due attention to the cooling effects of various anthropogenic emissions and the complex feedback loops; and that the models are merely speculation about the future which tend to minimise the uncertainties involved. They also argue that the anthropogenic emissions in total are very small compared to the natural emissions, and that it is arrogant of humankind to assume that their small percentage of emissions is capable of destabilising the global atmosphere. They submit that the IPCC reports are not truly scientific in that they present consensus views, and the language is long debated and negotiated (Priem 1995; cf. the work of the European Science Foundation; Boehmer Christiansen 1999).

This view is picked up by industrialists who see potential climate-change policy as having a negative impact on their economic growth

TABLE 2 The differing predictions for 2100 over 1990 in IPCC-1 reports

	1990[a]	1996[b]	2001[c]	Comments
Temperature increase (°C)	3	1.0–3.5	1.4–5.8	Because of lower SO_2 emissions in the 2001 report
Sea-level rise (metres)	0.65	0.13–0.94	0.09–0.88	Results of better models

[a] Houghton et al. 1990. [b] Houghton et al. 1996. [c] IPCC-1 2001.

(see pp. 120–5). In many countries the ministries of economic affairs tend to concur with their industrialists, who thus have an over-whelming influence on national policy. Most developing countries accept the IPCC conclusions, although there have been some controversies (see Box 20). At the same time, some environmental groups argue that IPCC is too cautious in its conclusions. It is also a fact that the predictions of IPCC reports keep changing; however, the IPCC provides explanations as to why its results are modified (see Table 2).

Predicting the future is not easy. There is probably no such thing as a business-as-usual scenario, where futures can be based on projections from the existing situation. This led the IPCC to take a new approach; they developed four possible future scenarios. The A1 scenario has rapid economic growth, low population growth, rapid growth of modern technologies and convergence in different regions of the world. The A2 scenario has a heterogeneous world with widely diverging circumstances in different parts of the world. The B1 scenario has a convergent world but with more emphasis on services and information, and a socially, environmentally and economically equitable and sustainable global society. The B2 scenario focuses on local and regional solutions, a diversity of technological change, moderate population and moderate economic growth. For each of these possible futures, different emission models were developed – in total 40 scenarios. In each of them it is possible to reduce greenhouse gas emissions, but the impact on society will be different (Nakićenović *et al.* 2000).

What does the new IPCC-I (2001) report then indicate? It indicates with some confidence that the emissions of greenhouse gases have increased without precedent, that these gases are known to have a warming effect, that the cooling effects of other emissions are less substantial, and that there is a strong likelihood that the changes in the atmosphere experienced so far cannot be solely attributed to natural emissions. The available evidence leads one to conclude that a climate change problem probably exists and is irreversible. However, there are grounds enough for sceptics to point to the wide range of uncertainties and state that the cause–effect relationship has not been proved.

The reasons for concern vary according to potential impacts. Unique, threatened systems are very sensitive to climate change and are already being affected. Extreme climate events are increasing, with serious effects on populations and environments. But the distribution of impacts is uneven; while relatively small temperature increases will adversely affect some regions, greater increases are expected to affect most regions seriously. The aggregate impacts may be negative or positive at lower temperature increases, but at higher increases they are expected to be deleterious overall.

SOURCES AND SINKS

The problem is made more complex by confusion concerning *sources* and *sinks*. Greenhouse gases are emitted by sources and absorbed by sinks. But sinks in the course of depletion emit greenhouse gases. Sources from industrial activities are relatively well understood concepts; sinks are relatively complicated.

Let us first discuss the sources of greenhouse gases. While there are a number of greenhouse gases, from the policy perspective attention is paid essentially to six. These gases are emitted in the energy sector through fuel combustion (energy industries, manufacturing and construction, transport, and so on) and fugitive emissions from solid fuels, oil and natural gas; from industrial processes related to mineral products, chemical industry, metal production, production and consumption of halocarbons and sulphur hexafluoride, solvents and other product uses; from the agricultural sector through enteric fermentation, manure management, rice cultivation, agricultural soils, prescribed burning of savannahs, and field burning of agricultural residues; and from solid waste disposal on land, wastewater handling, and waste incineration. In particular, carbon dioxide is emitted mostly as a result of fossil-fuel combustion and energy use in different sectors, and through waste incineration. It is also emitted when there is deforestation. Methane is emitted mostly from mining, enteric fermentation, manure management, wet rice cultivation and waste disposal systems.

What are sinks? As mentioned above, carbon and some of the other greenhouse gases pass through biogeochemical cycles. For example, carbon passes through terrestrial and freshwater systems, through oceans and the atmosphere. Human activities also have an influence on the carbon cycle. In order to have an accurate estimate of emissions it is important to have an assessment of how much the sinks absorb and emit.

When it became clear that few people had a clear idea of what sinks actually mean and how they contribute to the climate change discussion, the IPCC was asked to prepare a report on Land Use, Land Use Change and Forestry (Watson *et al.* 2000). Their report discusses the main issues in some detail and defines some of the key terms. It defines a *sink* as any process or mechanism which removes a greenhouse gas, aerosol, or a precursor of a greenhouse gas from the atmosphere. A *carbon pool* is a reservoir that can accumulate and release carbon. A *carbon stock* is the absolute quantity of carbon held in a pool at a moment of time. The *carbon flux* refers to the transfer of carbon from one pool to another.

The report calculates that 270 gigatons of carbon were emitted from fossil-fuel burning and cement production in the period 1850–

1998; in the same period, land-use change released 135 gigatons of carbon. However, the terrestrial ecosystems have also absorbed considerable quantities of carbon, and are seen as only a small net source of CO_2 in this period, but there is uncertainty regarding the exact numbers. The report also sheds some light on how land-use change as discussed in the climate treaties (see Box 10) needs to be developed. The key issue with sinks is how they are accounted for. In theory all plants and soils function as sinks, but sinks are not permanent: trees decay and die. How does one actually calculate these sinks? As subsequent chapters show, this concept became a centrepiece in negotiations in the late 1990s, and one of the most controversial issues being debated.

UNCERTAINTY ABOUT THE DISTRIBUTION OF IMPACTS

The IPCC reports also indicate what the changes will be for the globe as a whole. To explain what the averages mean in terms of regional and local climate is much more difficult. The key issue is where will the impacts be felt and who will be the most vulnerable.

IPCC-II (2001: 6) states: 'Vulnerability is the degree to which a system is susceptible to, or unable to cope with, adverse effects of climate change, including climate variability and extremes. Vulnerability is a function of the character, magnitude, and rate of climate change and variation to which a system is exposed, its sensitivity, and its adaptive capacity'. The report goes on to highlight the fact that since poor people have fewer resources and less capacity to act, they are the most vulnerable to the impacts of climate change and heat-related stresses. Noting that there are a number of difficulties in actually assessing the kinds of damage that might occur and the financial value of such damage, the report concludes that increases in global mean temperature would be likely to lead to net economic losses in many developing countries. If the temperatures rose marginally, there could be both economic gains and losses for the developed countries. If the temperatures rose further even the developed countries would experience economic losses. Slight temperature rises,

TABLE 3 Regional adaptive capacity

	Africa	Asia	Australia and New Zealand	Europe	Latin America	North America	Small island states
Adaptive capacity	Low	Low in S. Asia; higher in S.E. Asia	High except for indigenous people	High; little lower in S. Europe	Low	High except for some communities	Low
Vulnerability	High	High in S. Asia; lower in S.E. Asia	Low except for indigenous people	Low; little higher in S. Europe	High	Low except for some communities	High
Water stress	High	High	High	Variable	Variable	Variable	High
Food security	Low	Low	High, but at higher temperatures low	Variable	Low	Variable	Low
Loss of biodiversity	High	High	High	Shift in biotic zones	High	High in unique systems	High on coral reefs, mangroves
Impact on coastal communities	Significant	—	—	—	Significant		High
Disease	Increase	Increase	—	—	Increase	May increase	—
Extreme events	—	More cyclones	More cyclones	More river floods	More cyclones, floods	—	—

Source: Derived from Watson et al. 1998.

therefore, might increase income disparities between the poor and the rich. The loss of life and ecosystems is expected to be greatest in the developing countries. About 30 percent (1.7 billion people) of the global population lives in water-stressed areas today, and it is expected that their numbers will increase to 5 billion by 2025. This will affect the food production systems in these areas and the terrestrial and freshwater ecosystems. The impacts of cyclones and extreme weather events will heighten the stress of vulnerable people.

Who may lose more financially? Clearly the rich have more to lose. IPCC–II (2001: 13) reports that economic losses as a result of weather-related events have increased more than tenfold, from US$3.9 billion per year in the 1950s to US$40 billion in the 1990s, with three-quarters of the losses taking place in the developed countries. This monetary value reflects the increase in wealth, population and assets in the developed world. The irony is that as a coastal village becomes richer, the calculated losses of the village become greater, even though the loss to life and property may not be quite as physically devastating to the owner.

WHO IS RESPONSIBLE, AND WHAT ACTION CAN BE TAKEN?

The bulk of the anthropogenic greenhouse gases are emitted by the developed countries in the course of energy generation and use in the industrial, construction and transport sectors and through land use in the agricultural sector. These emission levels are closely associated with national developmental levels in most countries. Although on a general basis this is known, the national data is highly contested and depends on what is included and the methodologies used in measuring. The 1990 levels of the developed world as reported by themselves are shown in Table 4.

The bulk of global emissions are from fossil-fuel burning (coal, gas, oil) in power plants, industry, households and transportation. There are also emissions from mines and gas fields, rumination of animals (enteric fermentation) and wet rice cultivation, agricultural soils, field and savannah burning and waste treatment. The solutions lie in using better power-generation technologies, moving towards low- or no-carbon energy sources such as renewable sources and nuclear power (for those who find the latter an acceptable mode of power generation). The energy efficiency of industry can be increased substantially through better techniques. More efficient trans-

TABLE 4 Carbon dioxide emissions of developed countries, 1990

	CO_2 emissions (Gigagrams)	% of developed country total
Australia	288,965	2.1
Austria	59,200	0.4
Belgium	113,405	0.8
Bulgaria	82,990	0.6
Canada	457,441	3.3
Czech Republic	169,514	1.2
Denmark	52,100	0.4
Estonia	37,797	0.3
Finland	53,900	0.4
France	366,536	2.7
Germany	1,012,443	7.4
Greece	82,100	0.6
Hungary	71,673	0.5
Iceland	2,172	0.0
Ireland	30,179	0.2
Italy	428,941	3.1
Japan	1,173,360	8.5
Latvia	22,976	0.2
Liechtenstein	208	0.0
Luxembourg	11,343	0.1
Monaco	71	0.0
Netherlands	167,600	1.2
New Zealand	25,530	0.2
Norway	35,533	0.3
Poland	414,930	3.0
Portugal	42,148	0.3
Romania	171,103	1.2
Russian Federation	2,388,720	17.4
Slovakia	58,278	0.4
Spain	260,654	1.9
Sweden	61,256	0.4
Switzerland	43,600	0.3
United Kingdom	584,078	4.3
United States of America	4,957,022	36.1
Total	13,728,306	100.0

Source: The first National Communications of the countries to the Climate Change Convention excluding data from land-use change and forestry; data for 1990 and used in relation to the Kyoto Protocol (see pp. 44–9).

port, better public transport systems and fuel switching in the transportation sector are seen as options, as are changing the feed of animals and better animal management systems, moving to dry rice cultivation and methane recovery from landfills. The potential for action in the building sector lies in the design of buildings, and in materials and appliances used in them; transport, energy and material efficiency in industry, methane recovery from agriculture, energy supply and the efficiency of conversion (IPCC–III 2001).

REASONS FOR TAKING ACTION

Are there reasons to take action, and who has more reason than others? One can examine this in terms of the different regions of the world. For the small island states the answer is obvious. Their very survival is at stake and, hence, climate change is a serious issue for them. For the continent of Africa, the problem poses yet another threat to the water and food security of the people. The need for action would appear to be obvious for all the countries except perhaps South Africa, where policy measures may be seen to have a larger impact on its development process (see pp. 98–9). In Latin America and the Caribbean the richer countries face the same dilemma as South Africa; the poorer countries take a less ambiguous position. For China (see pp. 96–7) and India (see pp. 97–8), where per capita emissions and per capita income are medium to low, and both countries likely to be severely affected by changing climatic circumstances, their governments are taking a wait-and-see attitude in terms of climate policy *per se*, although both are pursuing their own energy and forest policies. For most developed countries, the science is evident; but so is the potential impact of taking action. The choice is not an easy one. Only the current US government has looked the choice squarely in the eye and decided that the effects of climate change on the country do not justify the effects of taking action to reduce the risk of climate change (see pp. 86–90). George W. Bush is gambling on being a winner in the climate change debate.

If one can divorce oneself from immediate national and individual interests in the global system, are there reasons for taking action? The answer is yes. Research shows that unique, valuable systems are likely to be badly affected by climate change and may be lost forever; these include glacier systems and coral reefs. Even if the distributive justice argument does not hold for many countries, the aggregate impact of climate change worldwide may be devastating, and large-scale discontinuities are expected. The continued emissions of greenhouse gases may induce such large-scale discontinuities as a shut-down of the thermohaline circulation or a disintegration of the West Antarctic Ice-Sheet (Nakićenović et al. 2000 [IPCC]).

INFERENCES

There is evidence of increasing emissions of greenhouse gases and of increasing extreme weather events worldwide. Is there a connection between the two? The IPCC argues convincingly that the past evidence of global warming and sea-level rise cannot be attributed solely to natural sources. Models that have combined the data tend to indicate that the increase in emissions has led and will lead to global warming. The model results tend to correspond with the actual data over recent decades. This gives confidence in the predictions.

As John Prescott, the Deputy Prime Minister of the UK, put it (2000): 'There will always be things that we do not fully comprehend, but that should not be used as an excuse for putting off action.... The overwhelming scientific consensus is that human activity is driving temperature changes and in due course will raise sea levels and give us more extreme weather. That means more floods and more droughts'. While some governments and environmental NGOs would clearly see climate change as serious, it is perhaps more telling to quote John Brown (Pew Centre/IHT: 2000), Chief Executive Officer of British Petroleum, who states: 'We can't ignore mounting scientific evidence on important issues such as climate change. The science may be provisional. All science is provisional. But if you see a risk you have to take precautionary action just as you would in any other aspect of business'. Even Dave Moorcroft (Pew Centre/IHT: 2000) of the World Business Council for Sustainable Development claims: 'The uncertainty surrounding global warming and the impact of climate change cuts two ways. On the one hand, estimates may be over-stating the risks. But then again, the risks may be even greater than imagined. This makes the whole subject resemble a high-stakes gamble. And, like any high-stakes gamble, climate change is serious business. What's more it cannot be resolved by any one nation working alone.' Some, seeing the problem in terms of winners and losers, would like to gamble that they will be the winner, on the basis of the current science. But it may be precisely those who think they will be the winners who have the most to lose if the gamble does not pay off. Who knows?

CHAPTER 3

THE CLIMATE CHANGE NEGOTIATIONS: FROM OPTIMISM TO PRAGMATISM

THE INITIAL OPTIMISM

Given the apparent seriousness of the problem of climate change, how did the global community go about dealing with it? The climate scientists had the issue on their agenda, and gradually, but with remarkable optimism, many of the developed country governments picked it up as a major problem calling for major action. This initial optimism was reflected in a number of high-level meetings, domestic targets and a draft negotiating text. The optimism also reflected a strong sense of responsibility towards vulnerable developing countries. However, as time passed, the lack of public support and the difficulties in actually implementing domestic targets became apparent. Developed countries began to back-track on their promises and the developing countries began to feel that they had been right all along in distrusting the North. The unfolding drama of the 1990s has multiple facets and dimensions. This chapter provides a brief chronological history of these events. Details in relation to various issues follow in subsequent chapters.

The first World Climate Conference had concluded in 1979 that climate change was a serious threat to humankind. In the decade that followed there was a handful of meetings to discuss the issue. At Toronto in 1988, 300 scientists and policy-makers from 46 countries met to discuss the issue and concluded that 'Humanity is conducting an unintended, uncontrolled, globally pervasive experiment whose ultimate consequences could be second only to a global nuclear war'. It called on countries to reduce CO_2 emissions by at least 20 per cent by 2005 in relation to 1988 levels as a first step. In the following year, Prime Minister Ruud Lubbers of the Netherlands invited some heads of state to discuss climate change, and it was at this meeting that the issue reached the highest political agenda. Later that year environment ministers from 67 countries met at Noordwijk in the Netherlands to agree to take action not only to reduce emissions of developed countries but also to provide assistance to developing countries to reduce their emissions (see Box 1).

Box 1   Agreements made at the Noordwijk Ministerial Conference, 1989

The political declaration at Noordwijk stated: 'Industrialised countries, in view of their contribution to the increase of greenhouse gas concentrations, and in view of their capabilities, have specific responsibilities of different kinds: i) they should set an example by initiating domestic action, ii) they should support, financially and otherwise, the action by countries to which the protection of the atmosphere and adjustment to climate change would prove to be an excessive burden, and iii) they should reduce emissions of greenhouse gases, also taking into account the need of the developing countries to have sustainable development' (Article 7). The text:

- Urged countries to adopt policies and measures, individually and jointly;
- Recognised the need to stabilise CO_2 emissions by developed countries at 1990 levels by 2000;
- Urged support for a further reduction of 20 per cent by 2005 by developed countries;
- Agreed that developing countries should also adopt policies and measures 'with due regard to their development requirements and within the limits of their financial and technical capabilities'; and
- Agreed that developing countries will need to be helped financially and technologically; and that additional resources be mobilised to assist these countries.

Source: Noordwijk Declaration on Climate Change 1989.

At the suggestion of the government of Malta, and with the support of many countries, the United Nations General Assembly decided to set up a process to facilitate the negotiation of a treaty on climate change. The mood was fairly euphoric; the Netherlands enthusiastically adopted a unilateral target to stabilise its emissions of carbon dioxide by the year 2000 as against 1990 levels (see pp. 92–4). At this time, the European Community also decided to adopt a common goal to stabilise its joint emissions by 2000 (see pp. 107–9). The less developed European Community members were not so enthusiastic, and it was understood that the more developed countries would take extra action to reduce the burden on these countries (see Table 8). Several other countries followed suit and, by 1992, 24 of the then 26 members of the OECD had domestic targets (see Tables 7, 8). The two countries that did not were the United States and Turkey.

At this time the problem was defined as one of emissions of greenhouse gases and depletion of sinks. The solution was therefore to reduce emissions and increase the sinks. The enthusiasm in Europe stemmed from the optimism that once a problem is defined, technologies can be found to deal with it.

Between 1990 and 1992, there were six meetings organised to negotiate the text of the treaty. There was heated debate on what sort of principles should be included. This debate was also taking place at parallel meetings in relation to the Earth Summit negotiations. The developing countries were in favour of principles, since this would decide how decisions were to be taken in the future. The developed countries were less in favour of principles, because they wanted to review each issue independently and not be constrained by any specific principle or precedent (see pp. 58–9).

There were also long discussions on actual commitments for the developed countries. At the time, many developed countries were in favour of ambitious targets (see Table 7). The NGOs and the scientific community supported such commitments. The United States government was completely opposed to taking on any quantitative commitments, arguing that this reduced its flexibility to act in the process (see pp. 86–90). The other countries wanted such commitments. Industry too opposed such hard targets (see pp. 120–5). Ultimately, the United Kingdom offered to draft a text that would express a quantitative commitment in ambiguous language, which in effect is no target at all (see Box 2). Considerable argument on the type of assistance to be provided to the developing countries followed (see pp. 63–77). Finally, in May 1992, the United Nations Framework Convention on Climate Change was adopted, and it was opened for signature at Rio during the United Nations Conference on Environment and Development.

THE CLIMATE CHANGE TREATY AND ITS PROVISIONS: VAGUE BUT SETTING A PRECEDENT

Like most treaties, this document too has a preamble, an objective, definitions, principles on the basis of which the responsibilities of countries are to be decided, a listing of obligations, the establishment of bodies to help with the implementation, and some other criteria.

In order to establish its legitimacy and credentials, the Preamble to the Convention states that climate change is a common concern of humankind, thereby avoiding references to politically charged terms such as global commons and heritage. It recalls principles in the United Nations Charter, the Stockholm Declaration on the Human Environment and the Ministerial Declaration of the Second World Climate Conference, and thereby establishes the need for such a global negotiation. It recalls that all states have the sovereignty to take measures within their own jurisdiction, but that they still have the responsibility to ensure that domestic action does not cause any damage or harm to other people in other countries. The Preamble also clearly notes that the largest contribution to GHG concentrations in the atmosphere has come from the developed countries, and that the per capita emissions of developing countries are still very low. It calls on all countries to adopt legislation and standards, but recognises that these will reflect the state of economic growth in individual countries.

As a critical step, the Convention divides the global community into three groups: developing countries, developed countries and former members of the Eastern Bloc. The obligations and principles are then allocated accordingly.

The treaty also defines a number of terms so as to clarify discussion. It defines the adverse effects of climate change as changes in the physical environment resulting from climate change which have significant deleterious effects on the composition, resilience or productivity of the system. Climate change is defined as changes that can be attributed directly or indirectly to human activity. Greenhouse gases are all gases in the atmosphere that absorb and re-emit infrared radiation. A source is a process or activity that releases these greenhouse gases, aerosols or greenhouse gas precursors, and a sink is a process, activity or mechanism that absorbs or removes such gases, aerosols and precursors.

Unable to define its specific long-term goal, the Convention agreed more general aims. The text states:

> The ultimate objective of this Convention and any related legal instruments that the Conference of the Parties may adopt is to achieve, in accordance with the relevant provisions of the Convention, the stabilisation of greenhouse gas concentrations in the atmosphere at a level that would prevent dangerous anthropogenic interference with the climate system. Such a level should be achieved within a time-frame sufficient to allow ecosystems to adapt naturally to climate change, to ensure that food production is not threatened and to enable economic development to proceed in a sustainable manner.

After much negotiation, five sets of principles were adopted in the treaty. These principles call on the parties to be guided by equity and the common but differentiated responsibilities of developed and developing countries, and ask developed countries to take the lead in dealing with the problem. The treaty requests countries to take the special circumstances of the most vulnerable countries into account. In line with a large number of modern environmental treaties, it recommends that parties should not wait for conclusive proof of the problem but should instead adopt the precautionary principle, which implies that since the problem is probably irreversible, parties should take action to anticipate it or prevent it from arising. It states further that each party to the treaty has the right to sustainable development

Box 2   The ambiguous text on targets:
what does this actually say?

The Climate Convention (FCCC) includes targets for developed countries. However, the wording is ambiguous. Thus Articles 4.2a and b read as follows:

2. The developed country Parties and other Parties included in Annex 1 commit themselves specifically as provided for in the following:

(a) Each of these Parties shall adopt national[1] policies and take corresponding measures on the mitigation of climate change, by limiting its anthropogenic emissions of greenhouse gases and protecting and enhancing its greenhouse gas sinks and reservoirs. These policies and measures will demonstrate that developed countries are taking the lead in modifying longer-term trends in anthropogenic emissions consistent with the objective of the Convention, recognising that the return by the end of the present decade to earlier levels of anthropogenic emissions of carbon dioxide and other greenhouse gases not controlled by the Montreal Protocol would contribute to such modification, and taking into account the differences in these Parties' starting points and approaches, economic structures and resource bases, the need to maintain strong and sustainable economic growth, available technologies and other individual circumstances, as well as the need for equitable and appropriate contributions by each of these Parties to the global effort regarding that objective. These Parties may implement such policies and measures jointly with other Parties and may assist other Parties in contributing to the achievement of the objective of the Convention and, in particular, that of this subparagraph;

(b) In order to promote progress to this end, each of these Parties shall communicate, within six months of the entry into force of the Convention for it and periodically thereafter, and in accordance with Article 12, detailed information on its policies and measures referred to in subparagraph (a) above, as well as on its resulting projected anthropogenic emissions by sources and removals by sinks of greenhouse gases not controlled by the Montreal Protocol for the period referred to in subparagraph (a), with the aim of returning individually or jointly to their 1990 levels these anthropogenic emissions of carbon dioxide and other greenhouse gases not controlled by the Montreal Protocol. This information will be reviewed by the Conference of the Parties, at its first session and periodically thereafter, in accordance with Article 7...

[1] This includes policies and measures adopted by regional economic integration organisations.

and that economic development is an essential prerequisite for taking measures. Finally, it calls on all parties to promote an open and supportive international economic system.

The next article describes the obligations of countries. It calls on all countries periodically to prepare national inventories of emissions and sinks, and to report on national policies and measures. It calls on all countries to cooperate in the field of science and technology, in relation to sustainable development, adaptation, education, training and public awareness. It requests the developed countries (listed in Annex I of the Convention) to adopt measures to reduce their emissions of three greenhouse gases (CO_2, CH_4 and N_2O) to 1990 levels by the year 2000 (see Box 2).

It calls on developed countries to provide 'new and additional' financial resources to developing countries to help them to meet the 'agreed fixed incremental costs' of preparing and complying with their national reports on emission levels and policies. The developed countries are asked to help especially those developing countries that are particularly vulnerable, and to transfer technologies to these countries.

All countries are obliged to prepare national reports on their emissions and projected emissions, and are requested to develop policies and measures to deal with these emissions. The Convention also requests all countries to cooperate in research and systematic observation of the climatic system, and to promote education, training and public awareness on key issues relating to climate change. The obligation on developing countries is, however, made dependent on help received from other countries (see Box 3).

In order to facilitate the implementation of the Convention, a secretariat was established to support preparations and to coordinate the activities of the other bodies. A Conference of the Parties was established to meet once a year to take relevant decisions after the treaty entered into force. There are also two subsidiary bodies that prepare scientific and technological advice and support implementation. To support the transfer of resources through grant or concessions, a financial mechanism was established and this was temporarily placed at the Global Environment Facility, a body created by the

---

Box 3   A key article on developing countries

Article 4.7 of the Convention (FCCC) specifies: 'The extent to which developing country Parties will effectively implement their commitments under the Convention will depend on the effective implementation by developed country Parties of their commitments under the Convention related to financial resources and transfer of technology and will take fully into account that economic and social development and poverty eradication are the first and overriding priorities of the developing country Parties.'

World Bank in cooperation with the United Nations Development Programme and the United Nations Environment Programme. In order to deal with questions regarding the implementation of the treaty, a multilateral consultative process was to be established. For dispute settlement, provision is made to allow parties to choose between arbitration, the International Court of Justice and a conciliation commission.

Parties are allowed to make amendments, add annexes or negotiate protocols to the treaty. Each country is allowed one vote (the European Union has the number of votes of the number of member countries; but either the EU votes or the member countries vote). The Convention can enter into force if at least 50 countries ratify, accept or accede to it; and no parties can make a reservation to the Convention.

The framework nature of the Convention, with its ambiguous principles and its weak targets and commitments, was such that most countries that considered the problem serious, perceived no immediate threat in ratifying the agreement. However ambiguous the principles were, however weak the wording of the target, the Convention still offered hope to all parties. Ratifications followed in swift succession, with the United States being among the first to ratify, and the Convention entered into force in 1994; the first Conference of the Parties (those who ratify) to the Convention was organised in 1995.

The Common but Differentiated Approach: Leadership Proclaimed

A cornerstone of the process was the offer of leadership by the developed countries. This offer appeared to consist of early reductions of emissions by developed countries, acceptance that the emissions of developing countries could increase, and recognition of the need to help developing countries to adopt modern technologies and adapt to the problem of climate change. At the Noordwijk Conference in 1989, the leadership concept was articulated in Article 7 (see Box 4). Some months later, the environment ministers of the UN Economic Commission for Europe concluded that they were 'ready to take a lead in the effort towards solving these problems and to assist developing countries in their environmental and developmental efforts'. A couple of months later, at the Second World Climate Conference in 1990, it was agreed that:

> Recognising further that the principle of equity and the common but differentiated responsibility of countries should be the basis of any global response to climate change, developed countries must take the lead. They must all commit themselves to actions to reduce their major contribution to the global net emissions and enter into and strengthen cooperation with developing countries to enable them to adequately address climate change without hindering their national development goals and objectives. Developing countries must within limits feasible, taking into account the problems regarding the burden of external debt and their economic circumstances, commit themselves to action in this regard.

These concepts were included in several articles in the Convention (see Box 4).

Partly because of the guarantees regarding their right to growth – later endorsed by Kofi Annan, Secretary General to the United Nations, in 1997, and by US President Clinton in his State of the Union address broadcast on 28 January 1998 – the developing countries were initially attracted to the negotiating table and have stayed there. Many developed countries indeed felt responsible for contributing to the problem and were confident that it was in their power to deal with it. This was not just altruism, since in the process the developed countries were able to move away from the concepts

---

Box 4   Leadership by developed countries

The Climate Convention (FCCC) states in Article 3.1: 'The Parties should protect the climate system for the benefit of present and future generations of humankind, on the basis of equity and in accordance with their common but differentiated responsibilities and respective capabilities. Accordingly, the developed country Parties should take the lead in combating climate change and the adverse effects thereof'.

Article 4.1 states that developed country parties shall adopt national policies and measures and that these 'policies and measures will demonstrate that developed countries are taking the lead in modifying longer-term trends in anthropogenic emissions consistent with the objective of the Convention'.

Several articles state that developed countries should assist developing countries in preparing inventories of emissions and adopting emission limitation and adaptation measures. It can also be inferred that leadership means accommodating the growth aspirations of developing countries. The Preamble states: 'the largest share of historical and current global greenhouse gas emissions has originated in developed countries, that per capita emissions in developing countries are still relatively low and that the share of global emissions originating in developing countries will grow to meet their social and development needs'.

---

of 'liability' and the 'polluter pays principle', from the role of 'bad guy' to that of 'good guy' in the international negotiations. There was also the promise of capturing new markets for new technologies.

THE TEMPORARY DIP

Soon after, economists and industrialists seemed to wake up to the potential consequences of embarking on such a negotiating process. Countries began to realise that the technologies may exist but were expensive, and that reordering society and its production and consumption patterns was going to be extremely challenging.

By 1994, the realisation had hit the Netherlands and some other countries that, despite the measures taken, stabilisation was not possible that year (see Table 7). In Norway, people felt that reducing emissions in a country that already uses a lot of hydro power and was fairly efficient would not be easy, and the government hoped that the international community would permit mechanisms that would allow a country to meet its target partly through the implementation of measures in other countries. Within the European Union, attempts to share the climate change target equitably among member states failed, and ideas to adopt economic instruments such as a carbon tax did not get off the ground (see pp. 107–9). New measures were added to the list of policies to be implemented. Research in the US indicated that although there was considerable potential to increase efficiency, the transaction and institutional costs of doing so would be heavy.

Meanwhile, industry and business groups began to get organised. The oil lobby resisted any change. Business interests were present in large numbers at the international negotiations, and were seen to be actively influencing them. Environmental NGOs had an uphill task. Although convinced of the need for action, the very abstract nature of the climate change issue made it quite difficult to convince the public of the need to take action (see pp. 116–19). Some scientists came out with tirades against the IPCC reports, arguing that they reflected political and not scientific assessments (see pp. 18–20).

All this led to growing political reluctance in Northern countries to take measures to reduce their emissions. When the Clinton–Gore team came to power in 1992, there had been hope that binding commitments would be possible. Gore's book *Earth in the Balance* had announced to the world his progressive views on environmental issues (Gore 1992). But although the Democrats were sympathetic, there was only limited support for measures from the Republicans. The thinking in the European Union was that legally binding targets were needed to mobilise governments into taking the necessary action. But the US government favoured talk about policies and measures rather than targets and timetables, in order to provide governments with the necessary flexibility. The EU countries, in response, refocused their efforts on policies and measures (Wettestad 2000; Yamin 2000).

In the run up to the first Conference of the Parties in 1995, the issue of Joint Implementation received a lot of attention. Joint Implementation was developed to allow developed countries to undertake projects to reduce emissions wherever in the world it would be cheapest for them to do so. This implies that they were not obliged to reduce domestic emissions of greenhouse gases, but could instead undertake a project in another country and would be rewarded by emission reduction credits. Barring a few Central American countries, most of the developing world opposed the adoption of this principle (see pp. 63–72 for details). However, since a handful of countries were interested in experimenting with this idea, the developing countries finally agreed to a pilot phase of Joint Implementation, during which no crediting would be allowed and countries could participate on a voluntary basis. This phase was referred to as 'Activities Implemented Jointly'. This compromise was unsatisfactory to economists, since there would be no way to evaluate how effective the crediting system actually was and how cost-effective Joint Implementation was going to be. There was no incentive for industry to take action since action was not linked to any direct benefits under the Convention. At the same time, the developing countries felt that the use of the word 'voluntary' had somehow undermined their unity, and they feared that if the pilot phase was initiated, it was more than likely that full fledged Joint Implementation would follow.

Many European countries felt strongly the need for legally binding targets and timetables to bring all countries under similar pressure to take action. The developing countries wanted this too, in principle, though some oil-exporting countries were afraid that this would seriously affect their export revenues. The more rapidly developing countries were also afraid that if targets were set for the developed countries, this would inevitably lead eventually to targets being set for them. At the same time, the small island countries, fearful for their very existence, prepared a draft protocol calling on developed countries to reduce their emissions of the three major greenhouse gases by 20 per cent by 2005. Environmental NGOs supported this position, and gradually pressure began to build within the G77. Although initially the larger and the more rapidly developing countries were suspicious of supporting the AOSIS protocol and the EU proposal, in 1995 the government of India drafted a document supporting the initiative, and within two days the bulk of the developing countries had rallied round the document. This was the birth of the 'green G77'. The OPEC countries decided to support the document rather than become marginalised within the G77 (Mwandosya 1999). This coalition between the EU and the G77 increased the pressure on the US. At that time, the US Presidency was inclined to agree but was aware that the Senate was opposed to the targets (see Chapter 6). Under pressure from the global community, and because of some apparent support from the NGO and research community in the US, the Clinton–Gore government decided to accept the decision, referred to as the 'Berlin Mandate'. This Mandate called upon the developed countries to adopt emission-related targets for specific time-frames. This was a major achievement, and the process of developing such targets was anticipated to last for two years. This achievement in terms of international process, however, was made against a background of increasing domestic fears of the consequences of adopting policies to deal with the climate change problem.

In 1996, the decision-making process moved more sluggishly, and the second Conference of the Parties had little impact. At the same time, the second IPCC report provided increasing justification for taking action. At this Conference, it is critical to note, the US suddenly changed position. It suddenly began to support targets, instead of policies and measures, as the most cost-effective way to deal with climate change. There was a flurry of research articles on emission trading (see pp. 69–72), and hasty discussions within the EU. No other country had experience of the concept, and even in the US the experience was limited to sulphur emissions. Nevertheless, a year later, the issue was not only on the agenda of all the other countries, but was adopted as an Article in the Kyoto Protocol to the Climate Convention (see pp. 44–9).

In June 1997, some months before the Third Conference of the Parties in December 1997, US Senators Byrd and Hagel introduced the Byrd–Hagel Resolution, which called on the US not to accept

Box 5   The Byrd–Hagel Resolution
and Senator Hagel's speech

On 12 June 1997, the Byrd–Hagel Resolution (Senate Resolution 98) was introduced in the Senate. It included the following:

'Whereas the exemption for Developing Country Parties is inconsistent with the need for global action on climate change and is environmentally flawed;

'Whereas the Senate strongly believes that the proposals under negotiation, because of the disparity of treatment between Annex I Parties and Developing Countries and the level of required emission reductions, could result in serious harm to the United States economy, including significant job loss, trade and disadvantages, increased energy and consumer costs, or any combination thereof; ...

'Resolved, That it is the sense of the Senate that –

(1) The United States should not be a signatory to any protocol to, or other agreement regarding the United Nations Framework Convention on Climate Change of 1992 in December 1997, or thereafter, which would –

(A) mandate new commitments to limit or reduce greenhouse gas emissions for the Annex I Parties, unless the protocol or other agreement also mandates new specific scheduled commitments to limit or reduce greenhouse gas emissions for Developing Country Parties within the same compliance period, or

(B) would result in serious harm to the economy of the United States; and

(C) any such protocol or other agreement which would require the advice and consent of the Senate to ratification should be accompanied by a detailed explanation of any legislation or regulatory actions that may be required to implement the protocol or other agreement and should also be accompanied by an analysis of the detailed financial costs and other impacts on the economy of the United States which would be incurred by the implementation of the protocol or other agreement.'

The United States Senate adopted this Resolution by 90–0 in July 1997. In October 1997, Senator Hagel made a speech to Congress stating, among other things: 'Many of my colleagues and I fear the current treaty negotiations will shackle the United States economy – meaning fewer jobs, lower economic growth and a lower standard of living for our children and our future generations. This treaty would do so without any meaningful reduction in greenhouse gases because it leaves out the very nations who will be the world's largest emitters of greenhouse gases, the more than 130 developing nations including China, India, Mexico, South Korea, and many others'. Senator Hagel goes on to argue that the treaty is flawed because it is based on inconclusive science, because it would compromise American sovereignty and because it would risk American security, since the US military is one of the major users of fossil fuels in the US.

Source: Congressional Record: 3 October 1997 (senate) page S10308–S10311; available at http://www.microtech.com.au/daly/hagel.htm

binding quantitative targets until and unless key developing countries also participated meaningfully in the negotiations, especially because of the increased costs associated with taking action for the US. This Resolution was adopted by the US Senate (see Box 5), and intensified the pressure on developing countries to agree to voluntary commitments.

This Resolution asserts that developing countries are exempt, under the Convention, from taking action, and that those countries that will be the largest emitters of greenhouse gases have been given no responsibilities. This is not entirely true. All countries are obliged to take action under the Climate Convention, but only under the Kyoto Protocol are the obligations of those developed countries who ratify the Protocol measurable as quantitative targets (see pp. 44–9). The Protocol does not imply that there will be no targets for developing countries in the second and following budget periods. The Resolution ignores the actual measures that are being taken in these countries to try and deal with energy conservation, promote renewable energy, and so on (see pp. 96–8). Besides, even though China and India may in the future have high total emissions, the per capita emissions of the United States are extremely high already.

In December 1997, the third Conference of the Parties took place in Kyoto. The European Union came armed with the decision of the Council of Environment Ministers of the EU countries that allowed it to negotiate for strong binding targets of −15 per cent by

2010 for all developed countries in relation to carbon dioxide, methane and nitrous oxide emissions in 1990. The US argued that it was not willing to go beyond stabilisation. Japan, as host to the negotiations, was caught between the need to demonstrate leadership in the negotiations, and the fear that being already a very energy efficient economy, such leadership would bring unacceptable costs and perhaps even unacceptable decisions, such as the building of new nuclear power stations. US Vice-President Gore went to Kyoto to push matters further and to table the US position. After hectic negotiations, primarily between the developed countries, and long after the official closing time and the homeward departure of several delegates on cheap tickets, the Kyoto Protocol to the United Nations Framework Convention on Climate Change was adopted.

COP-3: THE KYOTO PROTOCOL

The Kyoto Protocol presents a menu of policies and measures that all developed countries are invited to consider. These include energy efficiency policies, the protection of sinks and reservoirs, sustainable forest practices, afforestation and reforestation, sustainable agriculture, research and use of renewable energies, carbon sequestration, environmentally sound technologies, progressive phasing out of market imperfections and perverse subsidies, encouraging reforms in relevant sectors, controlling emissions from the transport sector, and controlling methane emissions. The Parties are requested to cooperate with each other in these areas. In addition, it is clearly stated that the parties should develop policies in relation to aviation and marine 'bunker fuels' – i.e. fuels used for international transport by shipping companies and airlines.

The Protocol goes on to mention the key element: the targets adopted. As a result of the negotiations, it was agreed that the developed countries would jointly reduce their net emissions (emissions from sources minus removals by sinks) of six greenhouse gases by 5.2 per cent in the period 2008–2012 in relation to 1990 emission levels (for the three additional greenhouse gases the base year was 1990 or 1995, depending on what individual countries wanted). The six gases

TABLE 5   The commitments of the developed countries under the Kyoto Protocol

	Commitment (% change in emissions)*
EU countries, Bulgaria, Czech Republic, Estonia, Latvia, Liechtenstein, Lithuania, Monaco, Romania, Slovakia, Slovenia, Switzerland	−8
USA	−7
Canada, Japan, Poland, Hungary	−6
Croatia	−5
New Zealand, Ukraine, Russia	0
Norway	+1
Australia	+8
Iceland	+10

* Commitment for the budget period 2008–2012; base year 1990 (1995 for the three new gases).

are carbon dioxide, methane and nitrous oxide plus three new gases – hydrofluorocarbons (HFCs), sulphur hexafluoride (SF_6) and perfluorocarbons (PFCs). The Protocol does not have separate targets for individual gases, but has a combined target for the basket of gases expressed in CO_2 equivalence. The individual percentage limitation commitments of the countries are presented in Table 5, and relate to the numerical quantities presented in Table 4.

The figure of 5.2 per cent came as a surprise to all. Many in the developed world had been predicting no targets; many in the developing world and the environmentalists were hoping for more ambitious targets. A developing country interviewee put it succinctly: 'Nobody knows why we agreed to a 5.2 per cent reduction'.

The negotiations had centred around the willingness of the US, the EU and Japan to take action. When Norway, Australia and Iceland demanded the right to increase their emissions, there was some hard bargaining, and these countries were eventually allowed to increase their emissions within limits, since a quantitative commitment was seen as better than none.

Although the EU has a joint target of −8 per cent, it appears more than likely that if and when it ratifies the agreement, the targets of member countries will be differentiated as shown in Table 6. These targets are based on an initial proposal based on a triptych method of quantifying commitments per country (see pp. 81–4), followed by some internal negotiations. France, with low greenhouse gas emissions because of its reliance on nuclear power, was thus allowed to stabilise its emissions in 2010. Portugal, Spain and Greece were allowed to increase their emissions given their relatively low level of development within the Union.

The term 'net emissions' allows countries to take into account afforestation, reforestation and deforestation and other agreed land use, land-use change and forestry activities since 1990 in meeting the quantitative commitments in Article 3. For this purpose, countries are expected to provide data regarding their carbon stocks and changes in them since 1990.

A certain degree of flexibility was offered to countries with economies in transition with regard to their base years and implementation. For the three new gases, countries were allowed to make 1995 the base year. By 2005, Parties are expected to show demonstrable progress in achieving the goals of the Protocol.

Article 4 states that countries may develop targets jointly; this Article takes the special situation of the EU into account, but is not limited to it. The Protocol allows countries to achieve their targets via the use of 'flexible mechanisms'. These include the mechanism of Joint Implementation, Emission Trading and the Clean Development Mechanism. Joint Implementation allows a developed country to invest in an Eastern or Central European country in return for emission reduction credits; this implies that if, as a result of an investment in such a country, emissions decrease in that country, the emission reductions can be credited to the investing country. Emission Trading was inserted at the last minute to allow the emission targets of

TABLE 6   The likely commitments of EU member states when they ratify the Protocol

	Likely commitment (% change in emissions)*
Belgium	−7.5
Denmark	−21.0
Germany	−21.0
Greece	+25.0
Spain	+15.0
France	0.0
Ireland	+13.0
Italy	−6.5
Luxembourg	−28.0
Netherlands	−6.0
Austria	−13.0
Portugal	+27.0
Finland	0.0
Sweden	+4.0
United Kingdom	−12.5
EU total	−8.0

* Based on Council Decision in June 1998; base year 1990.

countries, or 'Assigned Amounts' as they are called in the Protocol, to be made tradable. Thus if a country emits less than its assigned amount, it is allowed to sell the remainder to another country. The Clean Development Mechanism allows countries and companies from the developed world to invest in sustainable development projects in developing countries in return for emission credits.

The parties are also obliged to develop national systems for calculating emissions, to provide supplementary information to the secretariat in addition to what is required in the national communications, and to submit such information for review by expert review teams.

All countries, including the developing countries, were requested to create cost-effective programmes to improve the quality of national inventories using comparative methodologies, as well as national programmes to mitigate and adapt to climate change, and to communicate these to the secretariat.

Countries are expected to cooperate in technology, science and the development of education and training programmes. The developed countries are expected to provide new and additional financial resources to meet the agreed fixed incremental costs of developing countries in meeting specific obligations.

In order to facilitate the implementation process, the Conference of the Parties to the Convention can serve as the meeting of the Parties to the Protocol. The other organs of the Convention also facilitate the implementation of the Protocol. A key element of the Protocol is that its entry into force is delayed till at least 55 countries ratify the agreement, and these 55 countries should include countries contributing at least 55 per cent of the total CO_2 emitted by the developed countries in 1990 (see Table 4). This implies that, at least, the EU (with 24.2 per cent of the emissions), Russia (17.4 per cent), Japan (8.5 per cent) and some of the other smaller countries need to ratify; or the EU, Russia and all the other countries minus the US (36.1 per cent) and Japan. It is unclear what Belarus, Lithuania and Ukraine's role in all this is, because no numbers for 1990 were recorded for these countries in the document that provides the basic information for the article on ratification.

Some members of the EU had made it either explicitly or implicitly clear that they would be unwilling to ratify the Kyoto Protocol until and unless the US and Japan also did so. Japan had already felt, according to many insiders, manoeuvred into a position where it had to support tough targets in Kyoto, primarily because it was the host to the Protocol. Japan too was unwilling to ratify if the US did not do so. In effect, this all appeared to imply that the developed countries would be unwilling to ratify until and unless the key developing countries came into the open and stated explicitly how they would contribute to addressing the problem. This clearly raised the latter's hackles, as the leadership paradigm metamorphosed into a conditional leadership paradigm: we will lead as long as you promise to follow soon.

The exact rules and modalities of the three flexibility mechanisms were left for future negotiations, and it was unclear what exactly these mechanisms could achieve and how compatible they were.

POST KYOTO: COP–4 AND 5

President Clinton, who was under domestic pressure to secure the participation of developing countries, began to lean on these countries to take action. This led Argentina to try and put the issue of developing countries' voluntary commitments on to the agenda of the fourth conference of the Parties, hosted in Buenos Aires. But the item had to be removed following complete refusal by the G77 to accept it. Nevertheless, Argentina promised to pursue the matter in informal discussions. At the end of the second week of negotiations Argentina and Kazakhstan announced that they were in any case willing to take on voluntary commitments (see Box 6).

Other developing countries were annoyed at the disloyalty in breaking ranks, but most delegates realised that Argentina is quite rich: the meeting in Buenos Aires had amply demonstrated to most delegates that this was no normal developing country. And Kazakhstan, a former Eastern Bloc country, was not a member of G77.

Not much came out of the meeting apart from a Buenos Aires Plan of Action, which listed what needed to be done. At the fifth meeting of Parties in Bonn, little significant progress was made.

Box 6   Argentina and Kazakhstan

At the fourth meeting of the Parties to the Climate Convention, in Buenos Aires, Argentina announced its willingness to adopt a voluntary commitment. This commitment is expressed as a dynamic target based on the relation between emissions and GDP. The target is expressed as $E = I \times P$, where E is emissions measured in Carbon equivalents, P is GDP in Argentine pesos and I is the index value which is equivalent to 151.5.

Kazakhstan signed the FCCC in June 1992 and ratified it in 1995. It is a land-locked country with the world's ninth largest land mass, and a population of 16.7 million in 1990. Between 1990 and 1994, the economy of the country declined by 40 per cent. The National Communication (formal report to the FCCC secretariat) assesses that the negative impacts of climate change are likely to be much stronger than the positive impacts. Partly because of the decline in the national economy it was expected that emissions would decline to 45 per cent of 1990 levels by 1998 and would rise to 1990 levels by about 2011 and thereafter continue to increase. The country is proposing to adopt policies to increase energy efficiency and the share of gas and renewables in the power sector, to increase energy savings in the consumption sector, and to promote cogeneration. In August 1998 the government ratified the Kyoto Protocol. On 24 April 1999, in a follow-up to an announcement made by Kazakhstan in Buenos Aires, the Permanent Mission of Kazakhstan wrote to the secretariat of the UNFCCC asking for its status to be changed to that of an Annex I (developed) country without quantitative commitments under the FCCC. Since Annex I is not Annex B (developed country with quantitative commitments under the KPFCCC), this is a curious request and the implications of the request are not clear.

IMPLEMENTATION WITHOUT RATIFICATION

Despite the apparent deadlock, there was a silver lining. Political scientists argued that ratification was a mere legality; the international community could go ahead with 'implementation without ratification'. The Clinton–Gore presidency in the US was trying to support the process, despite opposition from Congress, and was trying to buy time by developing policies and initiating measures domestically. On 22 October 1997, Clinton himself said in a speech to the National Geographic Society: 'I want to emphasise that we cannot wait until the treaty is negotiated and ratified to act'. The EU countries were trying to lobby Japan, Russia and several other countries to set the stage for an entry into force of the Protocol by 2002.

Meanwhile, the goals in the climate change convention had still not been met by all Parties. Professor Bolin calculated that between 1990 and 1995, the EU had reduced its emissions by 1 per cent. Part of this decrease could be attributed to the merger of West and East Germany, and the closure of the UK coal industry. The unification of Germany led, on the one hand, to a higher emission figure for the unified country in the base year 1990 and, on the other hand, to the closure of a number of inefficient industries in East Germany, which had the immediate effect of reducing emissions. However, the emissions of New Zealand increased by 16 per cent, and the remaining OECD countries, except Switzerland, had failed to reduce their emissions. At the same time, the countries with economies in transition had recorded a decrease of 5 per cent. The emissions of all the developed countries as a group had fallen 3 per cent below 1990 levels (Review of the Implementation of the Commitments and of other Provisions of the Convention, FCCC/CP/1998/11), but there was no sense of euphoria or achievement. Eastern and Central European countries were by then deep in economic decline, and the EU expected its emission levels to rise in the coming period.

COP–6: IRRECONCILABLE BREAKDOWN OR MINOR HITCH IN A LONG PROCESS?

By the end of 2000, the ratification discussion appeared to have reached a stand-still. Only 33 countries had ratified the Protocol, and Romania was the only developed country listed in Annex B to have done so. Before the next round of negotiations, scheduled for November 2000 in the Hague, the US proposed in August 2000 that 'managed lands' should be seen as sinks under Article 3.4 of the Protocol. Almost all lands in the United States are 'managed' in one way or another, and these are estimated to absorb 300 million tonnes of carbon every year. Acceptance of this definition would imply that the US would have to do much less to achieve the 7 per cent reduction mentioned in the Kyoto Protocol. This was not acceptable to the EU and the developing countries (Grubb and Yamin 2001: 271).

Excitement built up before the sixth Conference of the Parties in the Hague, as the Dutch government was expected to invest time and resources to make the meeting successful. An ambitious plan of action was drawn up and there was considerable support for developing rules and modalities for discussing all the various flexible mechanisms in the regime.

However, as the meeting progressed, it became increasingly clear that the differences between the parties were deep. Furthermore, the consolidated negotiating text (a text that includes all the comments of all the countries and has a number of alternative wordings on the commitments and their details) was 150 pages long and extremely complicated. At 7.00 p.m. on the second to last day of the negotiations, the Chair of the Conference, Minister Pronk of the Netherlands, tried to bring new life into the discussions by introducing his own compromise text. His proposal was a package of measures that consisted of four sub-packages. The first contained measures in relation to capacity building, technology transfer and finance. The second related to the rules and modalities of the financial mechanisms. The third related to land-use, land-use change and forestry, and the fourth to policies and measures, compliance, accounting, reporting and review (see Box 7). Although the meeting continued all night and was extended beyond the last day well into Saturday, it was too late to secure consensus on the issues. The meeting was eventually suspended till mid-2001.

There was much speculation about the failure of the Hague. Some experts argue that this was because the compromise proposal came much too late and was not based on agreements with other countries, nor on previously negotiated text, nor was it presented as draft legal text. So negotiators did not know what to do with the series of points presented on paper. Europe was wrangling too much internally to be able to secure any progress externally. Furthermore, some felt that the Chair of the meeting was trying to meet the needs of developing countries without having first checked this out with the developed countries. Box 7 shows that the text indeed tries very hard to meet the concerns of the developing countries. It also appears that the issues in Chairman Pronk's proposal were not even discussed

BOX 7 Chairman Pronk's proposals

On 23 November, the Chairman of COP–6 came out with a proposal on:

1. Capacity building, technology transfer, implementation of Articles 4.8, 4.9 and 3.14, and finance. This included:

- The establishment of an Adaptation Fund to finance activities in relation to adaptation, financed by 2 per cent of the Certified Emission Reductions from CDM projects.
- The establishment of a Convention Fund for special help to Least Developed Countries (LLDCs) and Small Island Developing Countries (SIDCs).
- The increase of other financial resources to US$ 1 bn on an annual basis as soon as possible but no later than 2005 (and if necessary financed by a levy on Joint Implementation and Emission Trading).
- The establishment of a Climate Resources Committee to advise on existing bilateral and multilateral funding and on monitoring and assessment.
- Other provisions on Capacity Building and Technology Transfer and on the adverse effects of climate change etc.

2. Mechanisms:

This section talks about the management of the Executive Board of the CDM and that such a Board would need to be accountable to the Conference of the Parties/Meeting of the Parties; and that each Party may decide if a project is to be included or not; that the investors will exclude nuclear facilities from CDM projects; that the CDM projects should focus on renewable energy and energy efficiency; and that the developed countries will meet their emission reductions 'primarily through domestic action'. It also discusses certain rules relating to emission trading. In doing so it states, inter alia, 'Parties recognize that the Kyoto Protocol has not created or bestowed ... on parties ... any right, title or entitlement to emissions.... Parties recognize that the consideration of such commitments should be based on equitable criteria, common but differentiated responsibilities and respective capabilities'. In order to promote CDM projects in least developed countries, the proposal includes commitments on institution building in LLDCs, exemption from the adaptation tax and that the CDM projects should not use money from official development assistance.

3. Land use, land use change and forestry

The proposal suggests that the word 'forest' should be defined in accordance with FAO practice, and 'afforestation', 'deforestation' and 'reforestation' should be defined in accordance with recommendations from IPCC. In addition, for Article 3.4, grazing land management, cropland management and forest management and revegetation can be included. Since the inclusion of such a definition could make emission reduction requirements for certain countries irrelevant, the proposal suggests limiting the inclusion of sinks to 3 per cent of the Party's base-year emissions. Afforestation and reforestation were included as eligible options for CDM.

4. Policies and Measures, Compliance, Accounting, Reporting and Review:

The proposal includes a penalty for non-compliance and a subtraction of the excess emissions from future commitment periods; also that the party in non-compliance needs to present a compliance action plan. This is to be applied only to the developed countries. The proposal calls for the establishment of a Compliance Committee.

Source: Note by the President of COP–6, 23 November 2000.

---

in a tentative deal that the UK was trying to secure with the US on the final night of the talks (Ott 2001; Grubb and Yamin 2001).

Meanwhile, the new President of the United States, George W. Bush, made statements to the effect that he was not in favour of an agreement likely to jeopardise the US economy. In an unprecedented move, President Bush even stated that he was trying to see if it was possible to erase the American signature on the Kyoto Protocol. The political message that accompanies such a move was potentially devastating to the international climate negotiation process. Several protests from the EU and the German, Dutch, Japanese, South Korean and Chinese governments followed, but it was uncertain whether the US government would allow itself to be influenced by them.

An interim meeting was held in Ottawa between the EU and the Umbrella Group of countries, but did not yield much. A follow-up meeting in Oslo was cancelled. With President Bush's announcement that he wanted to withdraw from the Protocol, European leaders went to the US, but to little avail. In a desperate bid to try and create some degree of momentum, Chairman Pronk began to muster support from the rest of the world before the next round of negotiations.

The indications were bleak when the resumed Conference of the Parties began in Bonn in July 2001. And then, quite to the surprise of the outside world and possibly to the negotiators themselves, a compromise deal was reached. On 23 July, the Secretariat issued a press release stating that broad agreement had been reached on the following issues: a Special Climate Change Fund, a Fund for the Least Developed Countries and a Kyoto Protocol Adaptation Fund were to be established to help developing countries gain access to technologies, implement their commitments and adapt to the potential consequences of climate change. The press release stated further that the complicated issue of sinks was resolved as follows: 'The meeting agreed that the eligible activities will include revegetation and the management of forests, croplands and grazing lands. Individual country quotas were set; the result is that sinks will account for only a fraction of the emissions reductions that can be counted towards the Kyoto targets'. Rules for the flexibility mechanisms were adopted. It was agreed that under the Clean Development Mechanism, energy efficiency, renewable energy and forest sink projects could qualify, and that the developed parties were to refrain from using nuclear facilities in the CDM. The decision in relation to compliance was that a Compliance Committee with a facilitative branch and an enforcement branch would be set up, and for every ton that a country emits over its target, it will be required to reduce an additional 1.3 tons during the Protocol's second commitment period, which starts in 2013. These decisions were reached without US support. However, the Conference was unable to translate the political compromise into legal text. This was postponed until the next meeting.

BEYOND 2001: CRITICAL ISSUES AHEAD

In very simple terms, one can say that the climate change regime began with unprecedented enthusiasm and involved the entire global community (186 out of 194 countries worldwide) with a clear message that the developed countries would lead and the developing countries could follow. Despite the ambiguities in the 1992 Convention, the global community ratified the agreement en masse.

In 1997, the Kyoto Protocol was adopted with binding quantitative commitments for the developed countries. It then appeared that US ratification of the Kyoto Protocol was dependent on the so-called meaningful participation of the developing countries. The EU, Russia and Japan did not wish to ratify the agreement unless the US did so. The developing countries, with the exception of Argentina and Kazakhstan, were unwilling to demonstrate 'meaningful participation', as it was the task of the developed countries to take action first. Preliminary indications had shown that although some Eastern and Central European countries, the UK and Germany had managed to reduce their emissions of greenhouse gases, the rest of the developed countries' emissions were nowhere near stabilisation. Besides, the reductions in Eastern and Central Europe did not indicate a break in rising emission trends.

And then President Bush, in a reversal of his campaign agenda, and to the surprise of his own environmental department, decided to reverse the previous governments' policy decisions, and tried to seek erasure of the US signature on the Protocol, so that the issue of ratification would not arise. The President's oil-industry sponsors welcomed this step, but significant sections of US industry, engaged in renewable energy and energy efficient technologies in a number of sectors, would prefer to see a more proactive approach (see pp. 120–5). In an attempt to deal with the wrath of the rest of the world, Bush has since stated that he will make his own proposals about how the Protocol should be rewritten. As this book was going to press, no such initiative was forthcoming. Although it appeared as if many of the developed countries would hide behind the US position, on 23 July 2001 a political compromise was struck between all parties to the Convention, except the US. The US, it appears, has isolated itself.

Whether the rest of the world indeed has the courage to follow up the political compromise with legal text and to ratify the Kyoto

Protocol, now that so many agreements have been made regarding its implementation, remains to be seen. At the same time, one may also have some questions regarding the additional flexibility in the new decisions taken in Bonn in July 2001.

As we have seen, in the initial political process there was a clear commitment that the developed countries would take the lead, make room for the developing countries to grow, and even assist them to grow in an energy-efficient manner. However, there was now increasing fear that climate change would somehow be used to curtail the growth of the developing countries.

Although the developed countries got involved in the regime on the basis of the notion of state responsibility to take action, over time it appears that the states are abdicating their power on the issue and are trying to woo industry by creating an investment regime. They are thus transferring responsibility for implementation to the private sector through the various flexibility mechanisms. This can work only if the state indeed has power over the domestic private sector and the international regime has power over the multinationals. Comparison of the resources of the state and multilateral governance systems with the resources of the private sector indicates that such control is at best limited; indeed some would even talk of a corporate takeover of the public realm. Trusting the private sector to serve the interests of the public while maximising its profits may lead to substantial results, but it may simply be wishful thinking.

CHAPTER 4

THE KYOTO REGIME AND ITS CONTROVERSIES

Beware that you do not lose the substance by grasping at the shadow.

Aesop

The Climate Change Convention appeared to represent a fairly solid consensus; countries signed and ratified it in quick succession, and less than two years later it entered into force. Within the consensus there were controversies regarding principles, targets and assistance mechanisms. The Protocol, by contrast, is highly charged with political tension.

BEING PRINCIPLED ABOUT PRINCIPLES

In law, the word 'principle' has a very special meaning. Adopting a principle implies adopting a certain value that should guide the behaviour of states not just in the specific treaty concerned but also in relation to other treaties to be negotiated in the future.

In general, developing countries favour the adoption of principles in treaties. This is especially the case when they are less familiar with the details of the subject matter being negotiated, and they would at least like to have the rules of the game negotiated in advance. Once convinced that their contribution in causing the climate change problem was marginal, developing countries were quick to demand that the nature of the obligations of countries should depend on clearly defined principles. Developed countries tend not to be so enthusiastic about adopting principles, because of their 'open-ended' nature and legally binding character. They prefer to determine the nature of obligations on a case by case basis.

In the climate change negotiations that took place parallel to the negotiations at UNCED in Rio in 1992, the developing countries had a large number of principles that they wanted adopted. The developed countries resisted. This led to considerable debate. Through clever negotiations, the word 'principles' was excised from each of the principles in Article 3 of the Convention, and inserted in its title. At a subsequent meeting, the US delegation inserted a footnote to the title of the first Article stating that titles of Articles had been included only to assist the reader. The intention was clearly to suggest that the principles were merely values that could be taken into account, rather than standards that must be met. In the Kyoto Protocol, there is also clear avoidance of the word 'principles'.

TARGETS: HORSE-TRADING OR FAIR-DEALING?

Do targets really make a contribution to international decision making or do they hinder the process? Clearly, most developing countries are afraid of legally binding targets not only because of the implications for economic growth but also because they are not confident about being able to implement such goals. But the US and other developed countries are similarly reluctant.

Those who support targets argue that effective regimes are always based on monitorable targets. Tthey argue that targets chart a course of action towards an ultimate objective; they have a strong normative force and thereby guide behaviour through the creation of common expectations regarding the momentum of the regime; they can be used to claim political success and are, in fact, seen as news. They are also seen as useful in dealing with the free-rider problem and thereby create a level playing field. They send a signal to social actors and imply rewards for those who comply and punishments for those who do not.

Those who oppose targets believe that they may make a regime inflexible. With considerable foresight, Victor and Salt argued in 1995:

'If targets and timetables are negotiated now, the convention risks drifting away from the reality of what can be implemented and what will make it effective'. They argue that negotiating targets for individual countries reduces the focus of the regime to a numbers game where monitoring and accounting become the overriding concerns. It makes more sense to focus on effective plans and policies at the domestic level to curb greenhouse gas emissions. Others argue that targets are simply not a suitable indicator for managing systems holistically and sustainably. They may also not always be scientifically justifiable or socially defendable; their inherent rigidity may frighten off potential parties.

There have also been debates regarding gas-by-gas approaches when the targets are in relation to specific gases, as opposed to comprehensive approaches, when one target is adopted and applied to a basket of gases, or net approaches, when the target covers not just emissions but also sinks. Those who favour the gas-by-gas approach see the main advantage as the ability to measure and monitor the targets closely. Those who favour the comprehensive approach argue that choosing the gas they wish to reduce provides more flexibility to countries. Compromise decisions in this area have focused on comprehensive approaches.

Some argue that net targets are even more flexible while being much more accurate, since each country is evaluated on its actual emissions. Although the sinks approach is more accurate in theory, it is problematic in that the current state of knowledge does not allow accurate measurement of how soils, forests and oceans actually absorb and release emissions. However, supporters see the accounting problems as temporary, and argue that including sinks is in the long run more accurate and provides more flexibility.

The above discussion explains the ambiguous targets in the Climate Convention. But since the targets were not binding and there were no indications of follow-up targets at the time, the implementation of the norms was not encouraging (see p. 50–1). This led the EU and the developing countries to insist on binding targets for the developed countries in the Kyoto Protocol.

New targets were thus adopted in Kyoto. However, the targets met mixed reactions. On the one hand, the −5.2 per cent target for 2008–2012 for the developed countries was seen as falling short of what was necessary, and at the cost of a 12-year delay. IPCC (Houghton *et al.* 1990: xviii) had stated that if concentrations of greenhouse gases were to be stabilised at 1990 levels, emissions of carbon dioxide, methane and nitrous oxide would have to decrease by 60 per cent, 15–20 per cent and 70–80 per cent respectively. 'Stabilisation at any of the concentration levels studied (350–750 ppmv) is only possible if emissions are eventually reduced to well below 1990 levels' (Houghton *et al.* 1995: iii). This is especially so because there is an inbuilt inertia in the climate system, and unless substantial measures are taken fast the system is likely to become unstable. The Kyoto targets are very modest goals in comparison to what has to be achieved, and only a little better than what was subsequently agreed to in Bonn in July 2001.

The collective target was then shared among the individual developed countries. The EU received a −8 per cent target. However, since some EU countries received the right to increase their emissions, other developed countries also asked for such a right: Iceland claimed a +10 per cent and Australia a +8 per cent target. Developing countries and environmental groups were upset. It did not appear to be justified that Australia, Iceland, Norway, Greece, Spain and Portugal should be allowed to increase their emissions.

Another problem with the targets is that it is unclear what the precedent for other countries and the future is. As Figure 1 shows, targets have little to do with a country's economic status. The countries with economies in transition have relatively low economic growth and yet have accepted stabilisation and negative targets. Australia, Norway and Iceland have relatively high economic wealth and have demanded positive targets.

In addition to the fact that the country targets or assigned amounts appear to have been based on internal horse-trading between the countries, there are a number of loopholes in the agreement. As in the climate convention, bunker fuels (fuels used for international marine and aviation transport) are exempt from the Kyoto Protocol. Besides, the three new gases included in the regime were scarcely

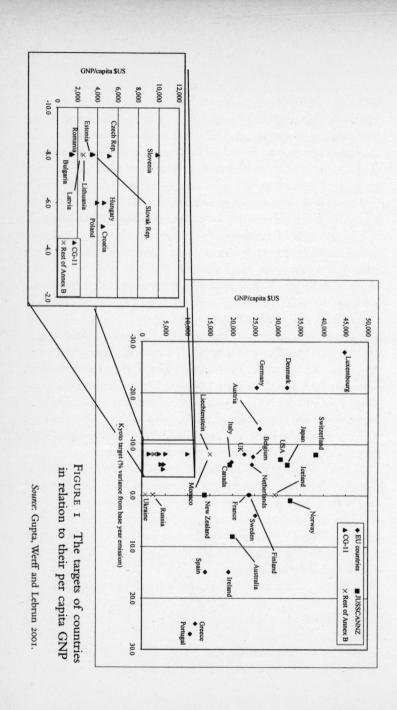

FIGURE 1 The targets of countries in relation to their per capita GNP

Source: Gupta, Werff and Lebrun 2001.

major offenders in the pre-1990 period, and the inclusion of flexible base years for these gases affects the actual significance of collective and individual targets. As Farhana Yamin put it: 'The new base year allowed Kyoto signatories the political kudos of agreeing larger numbers for exactly the same real effort' (Yamin 1998). The inclusion of sinks in the calculation of national commitments, which is not well understood scientifically in any case, also reduced the actual effort necessary to reduce GHG emissions. The potential for the developed countries to reduce their emissions in other countries through the use of the flexibility mechanisms reduces the actual effort taken in the developed countries to limit their own emissions. This was compounded by the problem of 'hot air' (see Box 8).

In January 1998, the US government tried to appease a home audience by stating that the factoring in of the three additional gases, the inclusion of sinks and the flexibility mechanisms would mean that their −7 per cent target was in effect much lower in relation to the three key gases (carbon dioxide, methane and nitrous oxide). The loopholes may simply imply that the targets don't go far enough. A much disappointed Ambassador T. Neroni Slade, representing a group of small island countries, concluded: 'And how can we be sure that these reductions will actually occur, or will industrialised countries continue to dump their waste gases into the atmosphere whilst "bubbling" their way to paper compliance?' (Slade 1998).

THE FLEXIBLE MECHANISMS: CARBON TRADING AND OTHERS

In the climate change regime there is much talk of 'flexible mechanisms' – mechanisms that increase the flexibility of policy implementation. Historically, the first flexible mechanism is the European Union 'bubble'. This provision allows the EU countries to have a joint emission target (Article 4.2a and b of the Convention). This in itself was controversial, since it was soon apparent that some EU countries would thereby have the right to increase their emissions of greenhouse gases while others would decrease theirs.

The three flexible mechanisms under the regime are Joint Implementation, the Clean Development Mechanism (CDM) and Emission Trading. All three mechanisms allow countries to use foreign emission reduction units (certified emission reductions [CERs] from the CDM, or Emission Reduction Units [ERUs] from Joint Implementation) towards meeting their national commitment. For a couple of years there was debate about what percentage of the national commitment had to be met domestically. While the developing countries, the EU and environmental groups were trying to keep the percentage high, industry and the rest of the developed countries saw no reason to limit the use of flexible mechanisms. This debate on the *supplementarity* of the mechanisms was resolved in the resumed session of COP–6 by substituting a percentage with the word 'significant': 'That the use of the mechanisms shall be supplemental to domestic action and domestic action shall thus constitute a significant element of the effort made by each Party...'

Joint Implementation

At the same time, countries began to realise that there may be cheap options internationally to reduce emissions: at least options cheaper than at home. This led to the development of the concept of 'Joint Implementation'. Developed country negotiators argued that Joint Implementation was a mechanism to allow an industry or developed country to reduce emissions wherever in the world it may choose to do so. This therefore allowed for cost-effective reductions. The economists found this proposal elegant, in that it allowed countries to seek the most cost-effective opportunities to reduce emissions, and since it is scientifically irrelevant where emissions occur, this seemed to be a wonderful opportunity to transfer resources and technologies to the South. The elegance of the idea was quickly grasped by the developed country governments as showing a critical, politically acceptable and environmentally defensible solution to the mounting costs of emission reduction.

However, the Convention was not clear in the distinction it made between the joint target of the EU and that of Joint Implementation. According to Article 4.2a, countries may implement policies 'jointly' with others, and Article 4.2d states that criteria for such Joint Implementation would be provided later, but the term was neither defined nor explained.

The majority of the developing country negotiators were not keen on this mechanism. While recognising short-term advantages, they were afraid that somehow it was neo-colonialist in nature, fearing that it would allow developed countries to continue with their extravagant, emission-intensive life-styles, avoid domestic responsibilities and the need to develop new technological and social solutions – such as alternative production and consumption patterns – and bypass the provisions for transferring resources to the South. They felt that the cost-effectiveness argument was based on grossly undervaluing the actual costs and exaggerating the benefits, while distorting policies and priorities in developing countries through the availability of resources to reduce emissions there. There was also fear that before long the developed countries would curb the progress of developing countries by imposing caps on their emissions, and hence on their economic growth. Environmental NGOs were also suspicious of the mechanism, fearing that it might lead to a transfer of Western life-styles to developing countries, and that this would in fact lead to emission growth everywhere: in the developed countries because they were compensating through investments in the South, and in the South because they had no quantitative commitments. Calculating what the emissions would have been in the developing countries was difficult. Joint Implementation would, in their view, lead to emission reductions only on paper in the developed countries (see Maya and Gupta 1996; Gupta 1997).

Nevertheless, under increasing pressure from the North, and perceiving the willingness of the Central and Eastern European countries and some Central American countries, developing countries agreed to a pilot phase of Joint Implementation in 1995 (called Activities Implemented Jointly), during which carbon credits would not actually be granted and countries could participate on a voluntary basis. This was despite the fact that the US tried hard to ensure that crediting was included, since otherwise business and industry would not be motivated to invest. There was an understanding that

the pilot phase would be reviewed before fully fledged Joint Implementation. Nevertheless, considerable suspicion remained in the
minds of many developing country governments. The Brazilian
government stated: 'as an alternative to the strict fulfilment of their
commitments, the developed countries have sought to re-impose a
reinterpretation of the concept of "Joint Implementation" in the
context of the Convention.... The reinterpretation ... advocated by
developed countries ... attempts to establish a "regime of credits"
through which they would compensate, by financing projects in other
countries, the non-fulfilment of the targets freely assumed by them
and which should be accomplished in their own territories with
regard to the reduction of greenhouse gas emissions' (Brazilian
position on Activities Implemented Jointly [1996–97], cited in Gupta
1997: 119–20).

By the time of negotiating the Kyoto Protocol, there were about
74 such projects, of which only 28 were in developing countries. Of
these 28, 18 were in Central America. The limited geographical and
sectoral distribution of these projects led an Indian minister to state
that there should be a proper spread and good evaluation of these
projects before fully fledged Joint Implementation should begin
(Venugopalachari 1997). Meanwhile, the 13 Eastern and Central
European countries with 46 projects were keen to convert their
experiences in the pilot phase into business propositions that would
facilitate their economic development. The combined support of
Eastern and Central Europe and the opposition of the developing
countries led to the adoption in the Kyoto Protocol of Joint Implementation as an instrument of cooperation among the developed
countries only. As of March 2001, there are 176 projects that purport
to be projects under the Activities Implemented Jointly scheme. Of
these, 43 are located in Latin America and the Caribbean, 24 in Asia,
14 in Africa and the rest in Central and Eastern Europe. These
numbers show an improvement in the balance of projects worldwide, as Africa had, for a long time, had only one project. They are
mostly energy efficiency, renewable energy and forestry projects.

At the resumed session of the sixth Conference of the Parties, it
was decided that the host country judge whether a project contrib-

utes to sustainable development; that emission reduction units from nuclear facilities not be used by investing countries; and that a supervisory committee be established to verify the emission reduction units generated.

The Clean Development Mechanism

At the same time, the Brazilian government was promoting the concept of the Clean Development Fund. Finances for this fund were to be generated through fines imposed on countries that failed to comply with their commitments. The purpose was to generate resources for transferring clean technologies to the South. But the developed countries were not keen on such a fine, nor were there any real quantitative binding commitments until the year 2012. This meant that such a Fund would have no resources for the next decade. During the process of negotiation, the Clean Development Fund metamorphosed into the Clean Development Mechanism – in essence, Joint Implementation with a new name. Article 12 (2) of the Kyoto Protocol states: 'The purpose of the clean development mechanism shall be to assist Parties not included in Annex I in achieving sustainable development and in contributing to the ultimate objective of the Convention, and to assist Parties included in Annex I in achieving compliance with their quantified emission limitation reduction commitments under Article 3'. Article 12 (3) states: 'Under the clean development mechanism: (a) Parties not included in Annex I will benefit from project activities resulting in certified emission reductions; and (b) Parties included in Annex I may use the certified emission reductions accruing from such project activities to contribute to compliance with part of their quantified emission limitation and reduction commitments under Article 3, as determined by the Conference of the Parties serving as the meeting of the Parties to this Protocol and be supervised by an executive board of the clean development mechanism'. The CDM is a voluntary tool and the credits can be banked (collected and saved) from the year 2000 onwards. However, in order to seek the support of the small island states who still opposed the mechanism, it was also decided that 'part of the proceeds' would be kept aside to finance associated administrative costs and the costs of adaptation projects in other developing countries. Many developing countries accepted this mechanism only with reluctance. They felt that while it would facilitate some degree of technology transfer, the mechanism had not been designed to deal with the shortcomings of the Activities Implemented Jointly mechanism in the pilot phase. Furthermore, it was later realised that the adaptation tax would in fact be a tax on North–South cooperation; that only when the North cooperated with the South would there be funds generated for adaptation. This has been a major source of irritation to the developing countries.

Another cause of concern is the notion of liability – what would happen if one of the parties in a CDM project was unable to keep its side of the bargain? Let us assume that a CDM project fails in a developing country because of shortcomings on the side of the developing country partner. Who is then to compensate the foreign investor? Will the developing country government have that responsibility? Minister Vargas of Brazil anticipated this concern in 1996 when he said: 'There is also a sense of urgency in promoting real financial and technological cooperation with developing countries as provided for in the Convention. Cooperation should not, however, be conceived so as to ultimately transfer to developing countries the burden of the fulfilment of Annex-I countries' obligations under the Convention'. Many developed countries saw acceptance of the CDM as positive. In a speech, Stuart Eizenstat (1998), then US Under-Secretary of State, observed: 'The Kyoto Protocol does not meet our requirements for developing country participation. Nevertheless, a major down-payment was made in the form of a provision, advanced by Brazil and backed by the United States, to establish the so-called "Clean Development Mechanism," which embraces the US-backed concept of "Joint Implementation with credit"'. Meanwhile, the acronym has become the butt of jokes. It has been referred to as the Confused Development Mechanism, the Carbon Dumping Mechanism, UN-Clean Development Mechanism and Complete Destruction Mechanism, because of its potential for misuse.

While environmental NGOs have been keen to limit the use of CDM projects to renewable energy and energy efficiency projects (see Box 16), business and many governments opposed such limits. For many developed and developing countries and for industry, CDM should also be available, they said, for promoting clean coal, gas-based and nuclear technologies. However, in July 2001, at the resumed sixth Conference of the Parties, it was agreed that the host country should decide whether a project is sustainable, that the developed countries are 'to refrain from using certified emission reductions generated from nuclear facilities to meet their commitments under Article 3.1', and that the developed countries were not to divert resources from existing official development assistance for CDM purposes. However, 2 per cent of the certified emission reductions achieved from CDM projects are to be reserved for the adaptation fund. Furthermore, the Executive Board that supervises the CDM would have ten members, one from each of the five UN regions of the world, two from Annex I countries, two from non-Annex I countries and one from the small island developing states. It was also decided that simplified processes for accounting credits for small renewable and energy efficiency projects should be decided by the Executive Board. A controversial feature remains the use of sinks. Under the CDM, only afforestation and reforestation projects are eligible for the first commitment period, but definitions are to be developed by 2002, and methods are to be devised to deal with non-permanence, additionality, leakage, scale, uncertainties and the socio-economic and environmental impacts, including those on biodiversity.

Emission trading

During these negotiations, another key development was taking place. Since the early 1990s there had been suggestions that a global permissible emission level should be calculated, and then divided among countries to trade between themselves. Such an idea presupposes that quotas are allocated to all countries on the basis of certain principles. In such a system countries that under-use their allotted quotas can sell to those who over-use theirs. If the principle is per capita equity, then countries with large populations get higher quotas. If the principle is existing emission levels of countries (referred to as 'grandfathering'), then bigger polluters get higher quotas. Schelling

(1997) explains that 'one cannot envision national representatives calmly sitting down to divide up rights in perpetuity worth more than a trillion dollars'.

Developing countries had stated all along that they wanted the allowances to be divided in an equitable manner – while per capita allocations were unacceptable to developed countries, who avoided the discussion. In Kyoto, however, at the last minute, an article on emission trading was included. Article 17 states: 'The Conference of the Parties serving as the meeting of the Parties to this Protocol shall, at its first session, approve appropriate and effective procedures and mechanisms to determine and to address cases of non-compliance with the provisions of this Protocol, including through the development of an indicative list of consequences, taking into account the cause, type, degree and frequency of non-compliance. Any procedures and mechanisms under this Article entailing binding consequences shall be adopted by means of an amendment to this Protocol'.

In the Kyoto Protocol, the right to trade emissions is granted only to those countries that have accepted quantitative emission commitments. The emission targets were assigned to the developed countries on the basis of hard bargaining between them, and they have the right to sell that part of their assigned amount that they do not use to countries that use more than their assigned amounts. Although at the time of the negotiations the developing countries were taken by surprise by this item, it was only much later that they realised its implications. The key point is that countries without quantitative commitments are not allowed to engage in trading. Clearly, since the emissions of developing countries are very low, they are allowed to increase their emissions. In contrast, Australia, if it can save on its emissions, can sell its excess to other countries, seen as extremely unfair by the developing countries. This is all the more so since countries such as Ukraine and Russia are unlikely to use their emission quotas by 2008–2012. If the US should decide to purchase the unused quota from these two countries, then it need take no measures at home; this is seen as 'hot air' in the system (see Box 8). Russia and Ukraine can encash their unused assigned amounts or targets; developing countries cannot. They can do so only against

Box 8   Ukraine and Russia: 'Hot air' or emission rights?

Ukraine and Russia are two countries in the middle of a raging EU-US controversy. Both countries successfully lobbied for a stabilisation target in 2008–2012. There is nothing surprising in such a target except that both countries are in a deep recession, and it is expected that they will not climb out of this recession in the next decade. It is thus expected that their emissions in 2008 will be substantially lower than they were in the base year. Under normal circumstances this would not mean much – except that the two countries were over-performing from a climate-change perspective.

However, with the introduction of emissions trading, this means that the excess emission entitlements may be bought by a third party. This, of course, only leads to an exchange of financial resources, and not to any significant additional reduction of emissions. This led Europe to object to the sale and purchase of the so-called 'hot air', so called because no additional reductions were created. Instead, these two countries could cash in on their depression. Russian and Ukrainian experts have been defending their countries' position on the grounds that this allows them access to financial resources necessary for their economy to recuperate and, ironically, to increase their emissions. It also provides the US with a relatively cheap solution to emission reduction. This angers developing countries, who feel they got a raw deal, since they had no entitlements in the first place to sell to the highest bidder. Meanwhile, Russia and Ukraine are waiting with their sales.... The price will rise as the target date comes closer.

actually implemented projects with measurable benefits under the CDM. This system also seemed to imply that instead of the largest polluters getting the largest bill on a polluter pays principle, the largest polluter also got the largest allotment of assigned amounts and could encash it if it chose to develop greenhouse efficient technologies. In effect the polluter got paid. At the resumed sixth session of the Conference of the Parties, it was decided 'to recognize that the Kyoto Protocol has not created or bestowed any right, title or entitlement to emissions of any kind on Parties included in Annex I'.

However, in the cold light of day, there are serious problems with Joint Implementation (cooperation within the North) and the CDM

(North–South cooperation). The CDM has become more expensive than JI, and perhaps Emission Trading, because of the stipulation that 2 per cent of the certified emission reductions should be set aside for adaptation and administrative costs. Furthermore, if the term 'sustainable development' is interpreted strictly, this may also raise the price of CDM projects, and there is an incentive for governments to define it so broadly that the projects can compete with JI projects. CDM does have an advantage over JI in that crediting can start in 2000, while that for JI starts only in 2008. Meanwhile, G77 efforts to ensure that the mechanisms are defined in similar terms have failed, since there is little support from other countries. The adaptation fund may suffer from lack of funds. If CDM projects are more expensive than JI projects, it is unlikely that the resources will be invested in CDM projects, leading to fewer resources for adaptation. It is also argued that 'these mechanisms effectively turn greenhouse gases into commodities, locking in existing North–South inequities in the use of the atmosphere and natural resources and opening up many new and harmful profit-making opportunities for TNCs [transnational corporations] – essentially creating a new market out of thin air' (CEO 2000).

TECHNOLOGY COOPERATION

The issue of technology cooperation is a sore point in relations between developed and developing countries. On the one hand it is very attractive for developed countries to gain access to new markets for new products. This leads them to propose that modern technology holds solutions for developing countries. But these technologies are expensive; this leads developing countries to demand technology transfer at concessional terms on the grounds that the North has polluted or that the North has the ability to pay. It is advantageous for the developed countries if the developing countries adopt modern technologies and emit less than they would have without them; this makes the global problem less serious. Hence, since the conference in Toronto, political and scientific declarations have mentioned the need for making technologies available to developing countries. The

Climate Convention specifically states in Article 4 that parties shall 'promote and cooperate in the development, application and diffusion, including transfer, of technologies, practices and processes that control, reduce or prevent anthropogenic emissions of greenhouse gases not controlled by the Montreal Protocol, in all relevant sectors, including the energy, transport, industry, agriculture, forestry and waste management sectors'. It goes on to state that the richer developed countries 'shall take all practicable steps to promote, facilitate and finance, as appropriate, the transfer of, or access to, environmentally sound technologies and know-how to other Parties, particularly developing country Parties'.

At the second Conference of the Parties in 1996, it was noted that hardly any technology was being transferred under this article and that countries should report on their transfers. Article 10c of the 1997 Kyoto Protocol repeats the importance of technology transfer and states that parties should:

> Cooperate in the promotion of effective modalities for the development, application and diffusion of, and take all practicable steps to promote, facilitate and finance, as appropriate, the transfer of, or access to, environmentally sound technologies, know-how, practices and processes pertinent to climate change, in particular to developing countries, including the formulation of policies and programmes for the effective transfer of environmentally sound technologies that are publicly owned or in the public domain and the creation of an enabling environment for the private sector, to promote and enhance access to, and transfer of, environmentally sound technologies.

Although there appears to be a commitment to transfer technologies, developed countries interpret this as being associated with the flexible mechanisms, while the developing countries see it as an independent commitment in which developed countries provide technologies at reduced cost. Developed countries argue that they do not own technologies: technologies are owned by companies, and hence it is necessary to find ways to encourage the market to participate, via, for example, the flexible mechanisms. This means that the private sector has to see some benefits in transferring technologies to developing countries. The Netherlands' government, for example, has set aside some funds to finance such transfers; in the case of other countries, it is conceivable that governments will allocate targets to domestic industry and other sectors within the framework of their national commitment. Companies with targets/quotas/allowances will then have an incentive to participate in Joint Implementation and CDM projects in order to gain access to the emission credits they need if they are to meet their allocated domestic targets. From the perspective of the developing countries, few real initiatives have been taken to implement the commitments under Article 4.5 of the Convention and Article 10 of the Protocol. This is the case not only in the climate change regime but also in others.

As a result the IPCC was asked to study the issue of technology transfer and make recommendations. The main barrier to technology transfer at concessional rates is the finance. The main barrier from the perspective of developing countries is the lack of capacity to identify and use the technologies, of an enabling environment, and of efforts to enhance mechanisms for transfer such as National Systems of Innovation, Official Development Assistance, the Global Environment Facility and the flexibility mechanisms under the Kyoto Protocol (Metz *et al.* 2000).

However, the problem is more political than institutional. As Junne (cited in Gupta 1997) explains, countries would like to promote their own technologies. This is a key barrier to the identification of the best technologies to address the climate change problem. Although countries have made resources available, it is unlikely that they will use them to transfer technologies made by competitive companies in other Western countries (see Box 18). Another key issue is that technologies that are successful in the West rapidly become cheap and affordable to some in the South. However, in the case of climate change, Western society is so locked into production and consumption systems that replacing these systems implies destruction of capital. Thus, they are unlikely to close down existing coal-fired plants in favour of renewable energy. This keeps the price of renewable energy systems high and relatively unaffordable for the South.

At COP–6 part two, the Conference agreed to establish an Expert Group on Technology Transfer, comprising 20 members (three from each of the three developing regions, one from the small island developing states, seven from Annex I and three from relevant international organisations). Whether the establishment of such a group will lead to actual results remains to be seen.

THE FINANCIAL MECHANISM

Another critical issue has been the financial mechanism. From the start of negotiations, developed countries have offered to make financial resources available to developing countries to deal with the problem of climate change, because of their historical responsibility for the problem, and their ability to pay. Hence, Article 4.3 of the Convention states that developed country arties 'shall also provide such financial resources, including for the transfer of technology, needed by the developing country parties to meet the agreed full incremental costs of implementing measures that are covered by Paragraph 1 of this Article and those that are agreed between a developing country Party and the international entity or entities referred to in Article 11'. Paragraph 1 of Article 4 includes the making of national inventories of greenhouse gas emissions, national programmes, the promotion of technology transfer and sustainable management of natural resources, cooperation on adaptation, integration of climate change considerations in national policies, cooperation in research, information, education and preparation of national communications. Article 11 of the Kyoto Protocol echoes many of these features. It states that the developed countries shall: 'Provide new and additional financial resources to meet the agreed full costs incurred by developing country Parties in implementing certain activities such as emission inventories and should provide financial resources, including for the transfer of technology, needed by the developing country Parties to meet the agreed full incremental costs of advancing the implementation of existing commitments in Article 4'.

To implement these provisions a financial mechanism was established. Many developing countries wanted an independent source of funding, and did not wish to be forced to ask the World Bank for more resources. They thus tried very hard to insist that there should be an independent financial mechanism. For most of the developed countries, this was unacceptable. They wanted a reliable funding mechanism where decisions would be based on sound economic principles. They also felt that in establishing the Global Environment Facility (GEF), they had in fact secured the ideal combination of the investment competence of the World Bank, the environmental knowledge of the United Nations Environment Programme and the practical development experience of the United Nations Development Programme. The developing countries disagreed; they feared World Bank dominance in the discussions. In the FCCC negotiations, the developing countries ultimately agreed because they feared that it was either the GEF or nothing. The first independent evaluation of this body was extremely critical, and the GEF has since tried to take the critique on board and respond to it. It has been decided that the GEF will become the permanent financial mechanism of the climate change treaties and decisions.

The developed countries had initially agreed to make *new and additional resources* available for the South. This refers to the fact that the resources should be over and above the existing commitment of developed countries to provide 0.7 per cent of GNP for ODA. Although some resources are being made available to developing countries, the essence of this promise has yet to be implemented. Existing aid is being diverted into tackling climate change, and the issue of agreed fixed incremental costs has been lost in the plethora of research on the subject, with no one having a full overview.

At the sixth COP, it was decided that there should be additional funding mechanisms with new, predictable and adequate resources, and that such funding should be reported on on an annual basis. A Special Climate Change Fund was set up to finance activities, programmes and measures related to adaptation, technology transfer, energy, transport, industry, agriculture, forestry and waste management, and to help oil-exporting developing country parties to diversify their economies. In addition, a Least Developed Country Fund was established to develop National Adaptation Programmes. Further, a Kyoto Protocol Adaptation Fund was established to be financed primarily by 2 per cent of the certified emission credits raised from the CDM to finance adaptation in countries that have become Parties to the Protocol. It remains unclear whether the resources will be forthcoming, since they are chiefly to be based on voluntary contributions. Even after UNCED, there were discussions on the need for financial resources. Only a fraction of the stated resources were ever made available.

Box 9   Articles to support adaptation
in the Climate Convention

Several articles in the Climate Convention provide support for adaptation. Article 3.2 states: 'The specific needs and special circumstances of developing country Parties, especially those that are particularly vulnerable to the adverse effects of climate change, and of those Parties, especially developing country Parties, that would have to bear a disproportionate or abnormal burden under the Convention, should be given full consideration.'

Article 4.4: 'The developed country Parties and other developed Parties included in Annex II shall also assist the developing country Parties that are particularly vulnerable to the adverse effects of climate change in meeting costs of adaptation to those adverse effects'.

Article 4.8: 'In the implementation of the commitments in this Article, the Parties shall give full consideration to what actions are necessary under the Convention, including actions related to funding, insurance and the transfer of technology, to meet the specific needs and concerns of developing country Parties arising from the adverse effects of climate change and/or the impact of the implementation of response measures, especially on:

(a) Small island countries;
(b) Countries with low-lying coastal areas;
(c) Countries with arid and semi-arid areas, forested areas and areas liable to forest decay;
(d) Countries with areas prone to natural disasters;
(e) Countries with areas liable to drought and desertification;
(f) Countries with areas of high urban atmospheric pollution;
(g) Countries with areas with fragile ecosystems, including mountainous ecosystems;
(h) Countries whose economies are highly dependent on income generated from the production, processing and export, and/or on consumption of fossil fuels and associated energy-intensive products; and
(i) Land-locked and transit countries.'

ADAPTATION

For many developing countries, adaptation to climate change is the key issue. The 40 small island countries, the 53 African countries, the coastal Asian, Latin American and Caribbean countries feel that they will face the brunt of the impact, although they were not responsible for causing the problem in the first place. Adaptation is therefore a key priority. The IPCC reports highlight the key challenges that these countries will face (see pp. 22–4). This is recognised in the Climate Convention, which states that special assistance must be given to the vulnerable countries (see Box 9).

However, very few resources have been made available under the climate convention and the Global Environment Facility to deal with adaptation. Only the Article on the CDM can potentially raise resources for adaptation. The Pronk proposal (see Box 7) and the political decisions taken at COP–6, part 2, also try to deal with this problem by the establishment of several funds (see pp. 75–7); but whether the resources will be forthcoming is questionable.

SINKS

A sink is defined in the Climate Convention as 'any process, activity or mechanism which removes a greenhouse gas, an aerosol, or a precursor of a greenhouse gas from the atmosphere'. Under the Convention, all countries need to report on their sinks in their inventories of emissions. Under the Kyoto Protocol, however, countries are allowed to include activities in relation to sinks since 1990 in their calculations of national emissions. Sinks are included in JI projects (in the Kyoto Protocol) and in CDM projects by decisions taken at COP–6 part 2.

Article 3.3 is unclear. Are changes in the sinks only in the commitment period (period for which the targets are valid) relevant? Or is this in relation to 1990 levels? Can one deforest in 2005 and afforest in 2008 and count the results only of the afforestation? What is a forest? How does one define it? When you cut some trees in a forest, is it deforestation? When you cut more trees, is that deforest-

Box 10   The provisions regarding sinks
in the Kyoto Protocol

Article 3 (excerpts)

'1. The Parties included in Annex I shall, individually or jointly, ensure that their aggregate anthropogenic carbon dioxide equivalent emissions of the greenhouse gases listed in Annex A do not exceed their assigned amounts, calculated pursuant to their quantified emission limitation and reduction commitments inscribed in Annex B and in accordance with the provisions of this Article, with a view to reducing their overall emissions of such gases by at least 5 per cent below 1990 levels in the commitment period 2008 to 2012...

'3. The net changes in greenhouse gas emissions from sources and removals by sinks resulting from direct human-induced land use change and forestry activities, limited to afforestation, reforestation, and deforestation since 1990, measured as verifiable changes in stocks in each commitment period shall be used to meet the commitments in this Article of each Party included in Annex I. The greenhouse gas emissions from sources and removals by sinks associated with those activities shall be reported in a transparent and verifiable manner and reviewed in accordance with Articles 7 and 8.

'4. Prior to the first session of the Conference of the Parties serving as the meeting of the Parties to this Protocol, each Party included in Annex I shall provide for consideration by the Subsidiary Body for Scientific and Technological Advice data to establish its level of carbon stocks in 1990 and to enable an estimate to be made of its changes in carbon stocks in subsequent years. The Conference of the Parties serving as the meeting of the Parties to this Protocol shall, at its first session or as soon as practicable thereafter, decide upon modalities, rules and guidelines as to how and which additional human-induced activities related to changes in greenhouse gas emissions and removals in the agricultural soil and land use change and forestry categories, shall be added to, or subtracted from, the assigned amount for Parties included in Annex I, taking into account uncertainties, transparency in reporting, verifiability, the methodological work of the Intergovernmental Panel on Climate Change, the advice provided by the Subsidiary Body for Scientific and Technological Advice in accordance with Article 5 and the decisions of the Conference of the Parties. Such a decision shall apply in the second and subsequent commitment periods. A Party may choose to apply such a decision on these additional human-induced activities for its first commitment period, provided that these activities have taken place since 1990...

7. In the first quantified emission limitation and reduction commitment period, from 2008 to 2012, the assigned amount for each
Party included in Annex I shall be equal to the percentage inscribed
for it in Annex B of its aggregate anthropogenic carbon dioxide equivalent emissions of the greenhouse gases listed in Annex A in 1990, or
the base year or period determined in accordance with paragraph 5
above, multiplied by five. Those Parties included in Annex I for whom
land use change and forestry constituted a net source of greenhouse
gas emissions in 1990 shall include in their 1990 emissions base year or
period the aggregate anthropogenic carbon dioxide equivalent emissions minus removals in 1990 from land use change for the purposes
of calculating their assigned amount.'

Article 7 calls on parties to prepare inventories of their sinks in
accordance with acceptable methodologies. This information is to be
reviewed according to the provisions of Article 8.

ation? If you just want fast-growing trees that absorb CO_2, how does
this affect biodiversity? The lack of clarity and potential for confusion are of concern to environmentalists and scientists.

Defining such terms as forests, forestry activities, afforestation,
reforestation, deforestation, carbon stocks, human-induced, direct
human-induced is a key challenge. Further questions concern what
methodologies should be adopted for accounting for emissions and
removals from sinks, especially in relation to which carbon pools to
include; how to interpret 'since 1990'; how to deal with the risks of
forest fires and pests, baselines, permanence and leakage; how to
ensure accuracy and verification; how to link the first and subsequent commitment periods; and how to ensure sustainable development (Watson *et al.* 2000: 3).

The Climate Action Network (CAN 2000) has pointed out some
significant risks in the sinks issue. They believe that definitions must
be centrally developed and not left to individual countries, in order
to avoid claims, for instance, that low shrubs are forests. They also
believe that a threshold as to what constitutes tree cover is inadequate
and that instead the IPCC should be requested to come up with
'biome'-based definitions. They insist that 'reforestation' should not

mean replacement by monoculture plantations of lands with other uses, including natural forests. They also argue that no credits should be given where natural ecosystems and biodiversity are lost or where land-tenure systems are disputed. Furthermore, NGOs argue that, although harvested wood products continue to store carbon, there is no real system for calculating and monitoring such harvested systems and that these should be excluded. Allowing sinks implies allowing a country to emit any amount of greenhouse gases as long as its sinks absorb the same amount. The problem is that most trees and plants will release the carbon stored in them if they are affected by pests, fire, drought, changing climatic circumstance, are cut down or eaten by animals. So this is not a permanent solution.

At the resumed session of the sixth Conference of the Parties, it was decided that land use, land-use change and forestry activities should be treated on the basis of 'sound science' with consistent methodologies. Thus, existing carbon stocks should not be included. When wood is harvested from a forest, the debiting from harvesting should not be greater than the credits earned on that piece of land. Different eligibility rules were adopted in relation to different Articles. Countries with quantitative commitments can use domestic 'forest management', 'cropland management', 'grazing land management' and 'revegetation' to meet their commitments in the first period, but must state in advance which activities they intend to use, and must demonstrate that these are the result of human-induced activities undertaken since 1990. Detailed rules regarding accounting were also decided. In the case of the CDM, only afforestation and reforestation can be included. However, in the first commitment period, such activities should contribute not more than 1 per cent per annum of the base year emissions.

EQUITY: THE TARGETS AND LEADERSHIP REVISITED

This brings us back to the issue of equity and the climate change negotiations. There are several possible approaches to dealing with the issue. The climate change negotiations could have kept liability and the polluter pays principle central. This would have meant that

Box 11   Possible equity rules

How should the climate change problem be solved? Who should do what, and when? Some (for example, the Brazilian government) suggest that responsibilities should be shared on the basis of current and historic emissions. Others suggest that each human being should have an equal right to pollute the atmosphere. Others argue against this principle. Still others argue that calculations should be based on different criteria. Suggestions thus far include:

- *Triptych approach.* Dutch researchers tried to find criteria for sharing responsibilities and dividing targets between countries. They concluded that the economy of each country has a different structure. In order to develop a system acceptable to each country, they identified three criteria: energy efficiency in energy-intensive industry; the structure of the power sector; and per capita convergence for the household sector. Such criteria would encourage the countries with energy-intensive industry to invest in energy efficiency. The special circumstances of countries in relation to the power sector are taken into account (Phylipsen *et al.* 1998). This idea was used to share responsibilities between the EU countries. Preliminary indications show that the OECD countries would have to reduce their emissions by 10–20 per cent, the Eastern and Central European countries would have to reduce by 30–50 per cent and the rest of the world can increase by up to 400 per cent, depending on how accurate the assumptions and data are.

- *The FAIR Model.* The Framework to Assess International Regimes (FAIR) model for differentiation of future commitments was also developed in the Netherlands. It incorporates a number of criteria to assess the implications of targets for individual countries. This model allows countries to make predictions based on different criteria. It is not prescriptive, but a research tool.

- *The CSE approach.* The Indian Centre for Science and Environment proposes a method based on converging equal per capita emission entitlements with restrictions on the types of technologies that can be promoted through the flexible mechanisms. This way they hope to introduce renewable energies on a large scale into the global economy, so that painful redistribution caused by converging entitlements is merely a theoretical threat, not an actual reality (Agarwal 2000).

- *The PEW approach.* A proposal of the Washington-based Pew Centre is that countries should be divided into groups on the basis of three criteria – GDP in terms of purchasing power parity, absolute cumulative responsibility, and current and future responsibility. The first group must to take action now, the second can take action now if they wish, and the third should take action now but using different measures.

The above suggestions are fairly idealistic. Negotiations thus far have revolved more around the willingness of countries to take on commitments than any real interpretation of what is fair.

countries paid in accordance with the amount of pollution they caused, and the money allocated to countries seriously affected by the impacts or those whose growth prospects were badly hindered. It might have developed in a leadership paradigm, where countries emitting high quantities of pollutants gradually reduced their emission levels on the basis of fair, predictable targets, and developing countries were given incentives to reduce the rate of growth of their emissions. The first concept was not even discussed in the international process. The second was heavily modified. Instead of negotiations focusing on the domestic implementation of reduction commitments by developed countries and an obligation to assist developing countries, discussion evolved into achieving domestic quantitative commitments perhaps through assistance to developing countries. The supplementarity discussion is now merely rhetoric. Not only that, the combination of quantitative commitments for some, and emission trading, has led to a situation where countries with the largest pollution levels get the highest quotas and can, in theory, even encash these. These developments do not augur well for the negotiation process. 'The challenge of addressing climate change raises an important issue of equity, namely the extent to which the impacts of climate change or mitigation policies create or exacerbate inequities both within and across nations and regions' (IPCC–III 2001). So how should the responsibilities be shared in the negotiation process between countries? Box 11 highlights some of the possible equity rules in discussion.

Paying lip-service to this issue, COP–6 decided that the developed country parties 'shall implement domestic action in accordance with national circumstances and with a view to reducing emissions in a

manner conducive to narrowing per capita differences between developed and developing country Parties while working towards
achievement of the ultimate objective of the Convention'.

CONCLUSION

The negotiations had started out with the hope that developed
countries would reduce their own emissions, and help developing
countries to leapfrog into the twenty-first century through technology transfer and financial assistance for reducing their emissions and
coping with climate change. Although the polluter pays principle
was not adopted strictly, the euphemistic rewording in terms of providing leadership and assisting developing countries came gradually
to gain some acceptance from the developing countries. As time
passed the paradigm of reducing their own emissions *and* helping
developing countries changed into reducing emissions *via* helping
developing countries and themselves. This made it easier to convince
the domestic audience in the developed world, but further annoyed
the developing countries.

Adaptation, although clearly a key issue for the potential victims,
and given a lot of room in the Convention, has received hardly any
funding. It was also for a long time excluded from the GEF; and
although it now comes under the purview of the GEF, the GEF has
yet to disburse funds for this purpose. Wherever developing countries
have tried to influence the debate, the developed countries have
managed to intervene with good negotiating tactics and redefine the
terms so that they no longer conveyed the developing countries'
meaning. There is now the political intention to establish a number
of Funds to support adaptation, but there is also many a slip between
cup and lip.

CHAPTER 5

THE PLAYERS AND THEIR CONCERNS: CAUGHT BETWEEN DOMESTIC OPPOSITION AND INTERNATIONAL COMMITMENTS

It is not only fine feathers that make fine birds.
Aesop

The climate change problem is like a game of chance. It is unclear how and when the climatic system will change and who will be affected. There is a lot of speculation as to who will win and who will lose. Clearly those who think they may win do not feel obliged to take any action, and feel that action can be delayed till it is clear that there is a chance they will lose. Some social actors in the colder countries feel that if the climate were to warm up a little, this would make life much more amenable. For the warmer countries, further warming and drying up of the water resources will only exacerbate existing circumstances. Again, how one perceives the risk is related not only to the physical nature of the change but also to the financial and technical ability to cope with it. Thus the Netherlands, which already has 60 per cent of its land mass below sea level, does not feel particularly at risk from further sea-level rise, since it has a method for dealing with it: every five years, the sea defences are surveyed, checked and strengthened if necessary. However, if the warm gulf stream were to become colder there would be much higher risks for the country. Risk is thus a question of perception.

The available evidence shows that the losers are likely to be those who are poor and live in marginal and vulnerable areas in both rich and poor countries. Thus those who live in coastal areas without sea defences are likely to be affected. Those who live on the banks of rivers fed by glaciers may be among the first to feel the impact of flooding. Those dependent on rain-fed agricultural systems will find that their crops are vulnerable. The poor and sick may lose their lives and livelihoods, but these may not amount to much in dollar terms.

The rich may be more willing to play the game of chance, but they have much more to lose. Their investments are of a much higher order, and if markets in the developing world weaken as a result of climate change, their profits may decline. Tourism and property values may be affected. Besides, in the event of a cataclysmic impact, no amount of calculated response will be of much help. However, responses to the problem are conditioned by domestic politics, which this chapter examines.

THE USA: BEATING ABOUT THE BUSH

The US is seen as a key actor in the negotiations; it sees itself as indispensable. The level of US emissions depends on how the emissions are calculated. According to an official calculation, the US accounted for 36 per cent of developed country emissions in 1990 (excluding emissions and removals by sinks; Report of COP–3, 1997). With about 4 per cent of the world population, it contributes about 25 per cent of global emissions. The per capita annual emissions are 20 tonnes, about five times the global average.

The US has played a curious role in the negotiations. American science has contributed considerably to the gathering of evidence in relation to the climate change problem. But while the main weight of US scientific opinion backs the view that there is a serious problem, ironically most of the dissident scientific voices are also American.

As far back as 1981, President Carter noted the seriousness of climate change and the need for responsible action. President Reagan, however, was not interested in the issue. Rising domestic concern following the severe US drought in 1987–88 led to the adoption of the Global Climate Protection Act, 1988, which obliged the President to prepare a plan for stabilising concentrations of greenhouse gases in the atmosphere. To a domestic audience, President Bush stated in 1988 that he was an environmentalist and that far from being powerless, the White House could take action. At the Noordwijk Conference on Climate Change a year later, the US representative, William K. Reilly, reiterated what President Bush had said: 'The United States will do its part.' According to the speech, Bush had amended the clean air laws to reduce air pollutants, had approved a decision to increase the corporate average fuel economy standards for automobiles, would support a worldwide phase-out of CFCs, would develop a national energy strategy and would support research.

> While it is necessary for all countries to work towards these goals, leadership by the industrialised countries is particularly important ... I wish to make it absolutely clear that the United States recognizes the special problems of developing countries in participating in the effort to address global environmental problems. We fully endorse, and even share, the aspirations of the developing world for economic improvement.

However, Bush was under pressure from the conservative Republicans not to commit himself to serious action, and by 1992 the government had decided to support 'no regrets' policies and measures rather than quantitative targets. 'No regrets' policies are policies that are beneficial for other reasons, so that if the climate change issue were to turn out to be relatively unimportant, such policies would still be justified for other reasons. When climate negotiations began in earnest, the first Bush administration was wary of two key issues: accepting open-ended principles (see pp. 58–9) and setting firm targets on specific gases (see pp. 59–63). The US government was becoming isolated in the wave of global agreement on the need for stabilisation in the developed countries. It was instrumental in ensuring ambiguity regarding both principles and targets. It was at that time unthinkable that the Bush administration would adopt carbon taxes, that is, taxes on the carbon content of energy; this would raise the relative price of fossil-fuel energy and lead to changes in consumer preferences. Bush had made an election promise of 'no new taxes'. At UNCED, President Bush reiterated that he would not compromise American lifestyles. At the same time, the government was trying to buy time by promoting a 'comprehensive approach', which would allow countries to have a single target expressed in CO_2 equivalence. This would allow flexibility in choosing which gas to reduce. They were also advocating that the comprehensive approach should include sinks. The US was opposed at that time to supporting technological and financial transfers to developing countries, although by early 1992 it was willing to contribute some resources to the GEF and to the US Country Studies Programme, which would help specific developing countries to prepare national inventories of emissions and assess impacts.

Nevertheless, when Clinton took over in 1993, he announced a political effort to stabilise domestic greenhouse gas emission by 2000 at 1990 levels. While industry became nervous, environmentalists and scientists were hopeful of action. But the Clinton administration faced tough opposition from the Republican majority in the Senate. Although Clinton had hoped to levy a tax on fuels, the Senate agreed to accept only a very modest tax. Since the price of oil then fell, the effect of this tax was scarcely felt. Later that year, the National Climate Change Action Plan was announced, which focused on voluntary action by industry and incentives for change.

It became increasingly evident that some market mechanisms would be necessary to promote cost-effective reductions worldwide. The government began actively to support Joint Implementation, and in 1995 reluctantly accepted that developed countries needed quantitative targets in the Berlin Mandate adopted at the first Conference of the Parties. In 1996, the US government prepared a draft protocol which was circulated during the negotiations. This contained elements of emission trading, the item that was later included in the Kyoto Protocol. Increasingly, however, some US industry began to feel uncomfortable at the pace of the negotiations.

This led Senators Byrd and Hagel to submit their resolution (see Box 5). The wording was clever and the House voted in favour of it. It was immediately clear that should a Protocol emerge in Kyoto, the government would be unable to ratify it. President Clinton began to lobby for 'meaningful participation' by developing countries. Vice-president Gore explained to members of the G77 the difficulties faced by his government at home (Mwandosya 1999). At the last moment, on 9 December 1997, the US agreed to go beyond stabilisation provided they got flexibility in achieving these targets. And the Kyoto Protocol was adopted.

Soon thereafter, support for the major elements of the climate convention was evident in a speech of the US Secretary of State: 'We need support for the Global Environment Facility (GEF), which embodies the partnership for sustainable development that was forged in Rio. This partnership is not helped by the fact that, in each of the last three years, we have fallen short of our pledged share to the GEF. We need to do better than that. We need to meet our commitments – in full – this year and every year' (Albright 1998). Although the Clinton administration gave the impression of understanding the key issues in the climate change agreement, some political economists pointed out that the Kyoto deal was faulty, because, although it gave flexibility to the US government in the short term, the allocation of assigned amounts and quotas to all countries was bound to become a sticky issue. American jurists and economists had long pointed this out. But while economists point to the flaws in the agreement and to the risks associated with implementing policies, the public may not be quite so indifferent. A Louis Harris & Associates poll indicated that 75 per cent of US voters supported the treaty (cited in the US Climate Action Network Citizen's Update, 16 January 1998, http://www.geocities.com/RainForest/6783/Kyoto USCANresp.html). A poll by the Mellman group indicates that 72 per cent of respondents would be willing to accept emission cuts by 2003 (Memorandum dated 17 September 1997 from the Mellman Group to the World Wildlife Fund containing the Summary of Public Opinion Research Findings). An Ohio State University poll indicates that 80 per cent of Americans believe that reducing air pollution will reduce global warming. But although many see the importance of action, few would support actual environmental taxes. And this remains a critical challenge. The first hundred days of George W. Bush as President did not, despite the number of environmentally unfriendly measures taken, dent his domestic popularity.

Now US emissions are reportedly 13 per cent higher than in 1990, and are likely to continue increasing. In order to achieve the target of −7 per cent, the US will need to take significant measures, especially since the US economy and its emissions are projected to rise considerably by 2012. In 2000 the US made a creative proposal to include all managed lands as sinks, but this proposal was not accepted at the meeting in The Hague (see p. 49). In mid-March 2001, the US government announced that instead of adopting policies to reduce emissions of greenhouse gases, the government was going to build new coal-fired plants. Emissions from the power sector are about one-third of all US emissions, and about 8 per cent of global emissions. US NGOs point out that investment in new coal plants will lock the country into a coal-based technological trajectory for the next 30–50 years (press release by World Resources Institute, 15 March 2001). They also pointed out that emissions from US power plants exceeded the combined emissions of 146 countries.

It is clear that in the perception of George W. Bush, the costs of taking measures to deal with climate change are much more than the costs of dealing with the potential impacts, and that he does not feel that the US owes other countries anything. This is not to say that there is not a large number of domestic actors in the US who feel strongly that, irrespective of the formal position of the government, social actors and alert business need to stay in touch with public opinion worldwide if they wish to be part of the global community. Three recent events have sent salutary messages to those who wish to listen: the US has been voted out of two key positions in UN bodies; and in the climate change negotiations in July 2001, the world showed that it is prepared to develop a consensus position that does not take the US into account. The international community is using its voting power within the UN to send messages. At the same time, there is increasing tension in the domestic context. The decision of a Republican Senator to leave the Republican Party in June 2001, arguing that the Republicans have gone back on their promise of being bipartisan, gives the Democrats a majority in the Senate.

Agrawala and Andresen (2001) argue that the US believes itself to be an indispensable party in the negotiations, but has indefensible positions.

THE UK

The UK contributed 4.3 per cent of developed country emissions in 1990, for the purposes of the Kyoto Protocol (Report of COP–3, 1997). The UK has prominent scientists in the climate change field, and has pointed out the seriousness of the problem since the 1980s. Margaret Thatcher herself is reported to have tabled the issue at a key meeting of the World Meteorological Organisation in 1986, and pointed out the opportunities and challenges for industry. The knowledge and role of British researchers in promoting the issue domestically and internationally cannot be overestimated. The storms and droughts in 1989–90 also put the issue on the public agenda.

But the United Kingdom was unwilling to go beyond a stabilisation of carbon dioxide emissions by 2005, as Mrs Thatcher made amply clear in the late 1980s. In 1990, however, it supported the European Environment Council's decision to adopt a combined stabilisation target for the whole of the European Community (see pp. 107–9).

In 1992, when the US remained reluctant to adopt a binding target, the UK drafted the text of the targets so that it continued to convey substantially the same meaning but without having clear legal force. The UK then settled for a domestic target of stabilising CO_2 emissions by 2000 at 1990 levels, reducing methane by 10 per cent and N_2O by 75 per cent. In CO_2 equivalence terms, this would imply a 5 per cent reduction in 2000 over 1990. In order to achieve these targets, the government aimed at using a Value Added Tax on domestic fuel and increasing industry fuel duties.

Mrs Thatcher also closed down the coal mines. An incidental effect of this was the reduction of GHG emissions, and the UK found, to its surprise, that it could exceed its targets. By 2000, UK emissions had gone down, and it is expected that it will be relatively easily able to meet its Kyoto commitments. The Labour government intends to get at least 10 per cent of national electricity from renewable sources by 2010. Prime Minister Blair has stated that 'I want Britain to be a leading player in this coming green industrial revolution' (*Time*, 23 April 2000).

The UK has always been fairly reticent about talking in terms of responsibility of developed countries, although it has recognised the arguments put forward by developing countries. While the other developed countries rushed in to prepare JI/AIJ/CDM projects, the UK government has taken a back seat on these issues, partly because they do not need to look for significant cost-effective options outside their country, and partly because they are sensitive to the arguments of developing countries.

The UK government has established a climate change levy, which entered into force on 1 April 2001. In order to avoid paying the full levy, 15 large energy-intensive companies have announced their willingness to take on formal greenhouse gas emission targets (www.press.detr.gov.uk/0102/0072.htm; and Reuters). The UK is said to wish to sell its over-achievements via emissions trading. Confident about the domestic position, deputy prime minister Prescott argued that the US position – that the science is uncertain, that reducing emissions would devastate the US economy, that developing countries are not doing enough, and that using sinks is not simply a ruse to delay taking action – was based on false premises.

AUSTRALIA, CANADA, THE NETHERLANDS, NEW ZEALAND, AND NORWAY: LEADERS TURNED LAGGARDS

Australia contributed 2.1 per cent, Canada 3.3 per cent, the Netherlands 1.2 per cent, New Zealand 0.2 per cent, and Norway 0.3 per cent of developed country emissions in 1990 (Report of COP–3, 1997). In the early 1990s these five had portrayed themselves as leaders in the negotiations. They had agreed to domestic political targets and were lobbying for major changes worldwide. Australia had a domestic target to stabilise non-CFC greenhouse gases in 2000 at 1988 levels, and to reduce CFCs to 80 per cent of 1988 levels by 2005. Canada, as host to the Toronto Conference in 1988, was instrumental in the adoption of the now famous Toronto target, which called on developed countries to reduce their CO_2 emissions by 20 per cent by 2005. The Netherlands, hosting the Hague Conference

TABLE 7   Leaders turned laggards?

	Domestic goals in early 1990	1992 targets	1997 targets for 2008–12[a]	Revisions since then
Australia	Stabilise non-CFC GHG in 2000/1988; reduce by 20% 2005/1988	All willing to accept stabilisation target for CO_2, CH_4 and N_2O by 2000	Demands and gets +8% emissions	Rumours that many of these countries will not ratify the Kyoto Protocol, following President Bush's lead; yet all have supported the political compromise reached on 23 July 2001 at COP–6, part II, which is not supported by the US government
Canada	Stabilise non-CFC GHG 2000/1990		Demands and gets a −6% target	
Netherlands	Stabilise CO_2 in 1994–95; reduce by 3–5% in 2000		Accepts a −6% target	
New Zealand	Reduce CO_2 emissions by 20% 2000/1990		Demands and gets a stabilisation target	
Norway	Stabilise CO_2 emissions 2000/1990		Demands and gets a +1% target	

[a] Base year 1990; for six gases.

of Heads of State in March, and the Noordwijk Ministerial Conference on Climate Change in November 1989, adopted a unilateral target to stabilise its emissions in 2000, and then the following year raised its aim to a −3 to −5 per cent target in 2000. Norway, too, was engaging in the so-called 'green beauty contest', stating that it was willing to reduce its emissions of CO_2 to 1990 levels by 2000. In 1992, at the time of the climate change negotiations, these countries all supported a stabilisation target, but because of US refusal, accepted a weakening of the text. In 1997, however, after heavy negotiations, at least two of these countries were able to lobby for and receive targets above their 1990 emission levels. Why did these countries change their positions? The answer probably lies in the fact that increased information about the consequences of climate change policy for individual countries had made them wary of taking on such commitments. After George W. Bush became President of the US, there were increasing rumours that Australia may follow the US and avoid ratification of the Protocol (see Table 7). At the same time, in July 2001 these countries all supported the consensus position developed at COP–6, part II, which does not include the US.

RUSSIA

Russia contributed 17.4 per cent of the developed country carbon dioxide emissions in 1990 (Report of COP–3, 1997). Russia has been facing major upheavals since the late 1980s. With the end of the cold war, and the break-up of the Soviet Union and the Warsaw Pact, Russia has searched for a new identity and ideology. The West wooed Russia and Ukraine with the ideology of the market mechanism and financial support, and Russia joined G7 to form G8. It also allied itself to the interests and aspirations of the West. In 1992, Russia accepted membership in the list of developed countries (Annex I) and the responsibility to reduce its emissions to 1990 levels by 2000. But the Russian economy was collapsing fast. In 2000 Russia's income and greenhouse gas emissions were substantially lower than in 1990. Nobody knows how long economic recovery will take.

Russia would now like to increase its emissions to 1990 levels, and argued in favour of this at Kyoto. Support came from unexpected quarters (primarily the US), and Russia succeeded in 1997. With the addition of emission trading, Russia secured the possibility of selling its unused assigned amounts to other countries in return for financial resources. Following Kyoto, an umbrella group was set up to find, *inter alia*, modes of East–West cooperation. However, although there was considerable enthusiasm for purchasing Russian emission reductions, the Russians were themselves more cautious;

they would prefer technology transfer through Joint Implementation, and would rather delay the use of emission trading.

JAPAN

In 1990, Japan's CO_2 emissions amounted to 8.5 per cent of developed country emissions (Report of COP–3, 1997). Japan is a very energy-efficient country and its economy depends on imported fossil fuels. It is also interested in becoming a major global power. These combined features led Japan to want to present a positive front at the climate change negotiations by arguing in favour of emission reduction, it also hoped thereby to find new technological options to reduce its dependence on imported fossil fuels.

In this mood, Japan offered to host the critical third meeting of the parties to the Kyoto Protocol. Having once committed itself, it realised that the Protocol could potentially bring un-implementable commitments for a country that was already extremely energy-efficient. Unofficially, word circulated that Japan was becoming nervous of the consequences of its generosity. But having made the offer, and faced with the ambitious EU goals for the conference, Japan found it difficult to backtrack. It even went so far as to accept a –6 per cent target for the budget period 2008–12; though it made clear that such a target could only be achieved through the establishment of nuclear power plants, which is extremely problematic given public resistance to anything nuclear since August 1945.

In 1998, the Japanese government adopted the Guidelines for Measures to Prevent Global Warming, which outlined the policies needed in the period to 2010. The government also adopted a Law for the Promotion of Measures to Prevent Global Warming. The measures adopted by the government include energy conservation in industry, transport, commercial and residential sectors and the promotion of renewable and nuclear energy. The government has developed voluntary action programmes to encourage industry to reduce their CO_2 emissions to 1990 levels by 2010. The practical domestic issues make it appear unlikely that Japan will ratify the Kyoto Protocol. However, if there is global support and unified action,

Japan may find it politically impossible not to ratify an agreement made on Japanese soil.

CHINA

China is in the curious position of being, on the one hand, a member of the Security Council, and thereby a powerful influence on global issues, and on the other, a member of G77, and thus a developing country. At the same time, the Chinese economy is developing very fast. With a population of 1.2 billion and high economic growth, Chinese greenhouse gas emissions are likely to grow fast.

Since the start of the negotiations, China has maintained that the responsibility for emission reductions lay with the developed countries. Such responsibility, however, should be accompanied by technology transfer. In 1992, China was reasonably satisfied with the climate change convention and ratified it in January 1993. In following years, China expressed its scepticism in relation to Joint Implementation as an instrument, and only reluctantly accepted a pilot phase in 1995. In 1996, the Chinese government submitted a list of technologies that it thought would help it to leapfrog to modern times. However, there was little response to the list from developed countries. Although China was a signatory to the Kyoto Protocol, there was initially enormous indignation in government circles regarding the adoption of the three flexibility mechanisms. Faced with the fact of these mechanisms, the government developed policies arguing that sinks should not be included in the CDM, but that nuclear power should be. These positions have been voiced since then at the negotiations and the Chinese government has also clearly stated that there should be no voluntary commitments for developing countries.

In the meantime, the domestic situation is undergoing a major upheaval. The structure of the government has changed several times. Since the early 1990s the power and industrial sector has been gradually liberalised, and small power plants and industries are being forcibly shut down. This leads to an increase in the efficiency of the power sector – since it is the small-scale power sector and the small-scale iron and steel, aluminium and cement industries that are most energy-inefficient. There is already evidence that the country has managed to ensure that economic growth is not accompanied by equal growth of GHG emissions; on the contrary, the government has been able to decouple its emissions from its economic growth. 'China has cut its energy consumption per unit of consumption in half since 1980. In other words, without these efforts, China's CO_2 emissions in 1997 would have been 432.32 MtC higher, or more than 50 per cent higher than its actual emissions' (Zhang 1999: 55; see also Gupta *et al.* 2001b). This means that the society is modernising very fast. The driving force behind this is not climate change, but liberalisation and the need to deal with local pollution. Nevertheless, this has benefits in terms of climate change. Chinese experts argue that they should not have to take on any emission restrictions until they are at least a relatively rich country, which they expect will happen in the middle of the twenty-first century.

INDIA

India is a developing country with a population of almost 1 billion. Its economy, although not developing quite as fast as that of China, is growing rapidly. India has an influential position in the G77. In 1989, an Indian minister stated: 'It may be counter-productive to lay down targets for countries which are still striving to raise the living conditions of their masses. It may be equally counter-productive to reach agreements to combat climate change, without devising mechanisms to ensure global participation' (Prasad 1990). Since then, the Indian government's position has been that its per capita emissions are nominal, and that it is the responsibility of the developed world to take action (cf. Dasgupta 1994). It ratified the Convention fairly quickly. However, India has neither signed nor ratified the Kyoto Protocol. Like China, India has been sceptical with regard to Joint Implementation and the flexibility mechanisms. An Indian negotiator argues that 'the South was strident about the emission trading and transnational "carbon offset" projects. It feared that the rules for "buying" and "selling" greenhouse gas allowances could very well gift rights to entitlements, freezing North–South disparities'. He goes on to say that 'the North's current occupation of environmental space must not lead to property rights.... The Seattle and Hague conferences show how utilitarian rationalism is thin ice for sustaining North–South dialogue' (Sharma 2001).

Faced with a fait accompli, however, and partly because of high-level visits from US Secretary of State Madeleine Albright and President Clinton, the CDM is now on the agenda of several Indian government ministries and company boardrooms. The domestic discussion has taken off, but there appear to be no easy answers. The choices in the energy field are woefully problematic. While the use of coal is now questioned, large-scale hydropower has also faced global and local opposition, as has nuclear power. Renewable energy, seen as far too expensive in the developed countries, remains unaffordable in the developing countries. Since 1990 the government has been liberalising the energy and industry sector. India is the only country in the world with a fully fledged ministry promoting renewable energy. It is already the world's fifth largest producer of wind energy. The government has published a Bill proposing that renewable energy should provide 10 per cent of electricity in India by 2012. An Energy Efficiency Bill is also expected to be adopted. Research indicates that India is on the way to decoupling its electricity production from emissions, and is gradually becoming energy efficient. There is still considerable potential to improve the energy efficiency of the economy and there are domestic reasons to pursue this policy. The potential impact of climate change on India is dramatic. The Himalayan glaciers are vulnerable and already melting. Temperatures are expected to rise by 1 per cent on average, and monsoons to decline, leading to a significant reduction in water resources. Low-lying coastal areas are vulnerable to typhoons and rising sea-levels. It is also expected that agricultural production will decrease and vector-borne diseases increase.

South Africa

South Africa has only recently begun to participate in international negotiations, having been for a long time isolated from the rest of the global community. Like China and India it has high total greenhouse gas emissions, but unlike them it has very high per capita emissions. Despite its appearance as a highly industrialised country, its per capita income is quite low. The high per capita emissions of South Africa reflect a highly industrialised sector using energy mostly from fossil fuels. Coal-fired plants are the major emitters of greenhouse gases, and the huge mining industry is also responsible for large emissions. The government of South Africa is acutely aware that it is one of the largest polluters in the world; but it is also aware of the lack of development in large tracts of South Africa. Arguing that it is a developing country and that its political strategy is determined first at national level, then at the level of SADC, then at the level of Africa, then at the level of the G77, it states that it is willing to participate in the flexibility mechanisms and utilise opportunities for technology cooperation. The power sector is in the hands of ESCOM, a parastatal company said to be the fifth largest in the world. ESCOM has built up its reputation and technological and financial power on coal and is reluctant to change its resource base. Moreover it has considerable influence on government policy, which at this moment faces major challenges from competing social issues. There is a National Committee on Climate Change that prepares national strategy, but the government has, like other developing countries, adopted a defensive role in international negotiations.

SUMMARY

An examination of the domestic situation in all these countries reveals little difference in their aspirations. While developing countries are seen as the problem because they do not wish to tread the path of sustainable development but opt instead for growth, it is becoming increasingly clear that for most developed countries, too, economic growth is the key motivating factor. Norway and Australia are among the richest countries and yet the drive to be richer makes them demand targets to increase emissions. The US is not only rich, but has huge opportunities for emission reduction, but does not wish to risk the employment opportunities of its people. Although the EU has tried to take a lead, it does not dare to strike out alone, and member countries may individually be quite relieved. Hence the consensus of complacency. At the same time, although developing countries are being defensive in the negotiations, they are taking measures: even if climate change is not the motivating factor, they are being influenced by the climate discussions and other global trends. As John Prescott recognises: 'the fact is that developing countries already are taking a lot of action that will limit their emissions growth. For example, it has been estimated that China's emissions would have been 50 per cent higher without energy reforms' (Prescott 2000).

CHAPTER 6

THE GAME OF COALITIONS

Countries form coalitions. The world groups and re-groups itself into formations of countries that have similar interests. As noted in previous chapters, the world has essentially divided itself into two groups – the developed and the developing. This division is reflected in the division of responsibilities under the Convention and the Protocol. Each group has further divided itself into smaller, more distinct groups: there are groups within groups. This chapter discusses some of these coalitions and the role they play in the process of negotiation. As will become increasingly clear, countries tend to coalesce along regional and political lines, and these co-alitions do not necessarily reflect each individual country's national interests.

Clearly it would be difficult for 190 countries to negotiate if they did not form groups. Coalitions help to reduce the transaction costs of conveying a message to the international community, and they tend to reduce the free-rider problem. Countries also increase their negotiating power through making coalitions.

Coalitions may be formed on the basis of a common institutional framework and legal identity, such as the European Union, of geography, such as the Organisation of African Unity, of perceived common interests, such as JUSSCANNZ (see below) or predicament, such as the Alliance of Small Island States.

THE NORTH–SOUTH DICHOTOMY

At a very abstract level, negotiations take place between the North and the South. The North is represented by what is referred to as Annex I (developed countries) or Annex B (developed countries with specific quantitative commitments) in the climate change negotiations (see Chapter 3); the rest of the world is outside these Annexes. The South is generally represented by the G77. International negotiations within the UN, the WTO and GATT normally follow such divisions, which tend to have a strong force of precedent.

The G77 was established in 1964 to help the South to group and negotiate. It has at present 133 members, of which 130 are active nation states. It has a rotating leadership from the different continents, and the chair holds the position for a year. Resources limit the number of countries volunteering to lead the G77: Nigeria chaired in 2000 and Iran in 2001. The lack of financial resources and the diverse membership have made it difficult for the G77 to develop a clear, consistent negotiating strategy in relation to the wide variety of issues on the international table. The G77 has five chapters, located in Rome, Paris, Nairobi, Washington and Vienna, and held its first ever global summit in 2000 (see Box 12).

However, in the division of the world into developed and developing, the group 'developing' is a sort of residual category. This group consists of 153 countries, of which only 130 are G77 countries. Twenty-three countries belong neither to the North nor to the G77, but are clubbed together with the South. These include the new OECD countries, Mexico and South Korea; the former Eastern Bloc countries, Albania, Armenia, Azerbaijan, Georgia, Kazakhstan, Kyrgyzstan, Macedonia, Moldova, Tajikistan, Uzbekistan, the Federal Republic of Yugoslavia; the island states, Cook Islands, Kiribati, Nauru, Niue, Palau and Tuvalu; plus Andorra, Israel, the Holy See and San Marino. The loyalties of these countries are uncertain. They have varying bonds with the South and with the North. How alliances will develop in the future is uncertain. Kazakhstan made clear at the Buenos Aires negotiations that it wished to ally itself with the developed countries (see Box 6).

BOX 12   The G77 and its first summit in 2000

In 2000, the Group of 77 had its first ever global summit. There it reiterated that its purpose is to 'map out a better future for our countries and peoples and to work towards the establishment of an international economic system which will be just and democratic'. The heads of state from the developing countries made a list of all the key issues facing them. Environmental issues got little coverage. The summit stated:

- 'While recognising the value of environmental protection, labour standards, intellectual property protection, indigenous innovation and local community, sound macroeconomic management and promotion and protection of all universally recognised human rights and fundamental freedoms, including the right to development, and the treatment of each issue in its competent international organisation, we reject all attempts to use these issues as conditionalities for restricting market access or aid and technology flows to developing countries.
- 'We note with deep concern the continuing decline of official development assistance (ODA), which has adversely affected development activities in the developing countries, in particular the LDCs, and we therefore urge developed countries that have not yet done so to act immediately to honour their commitments of directing 0.7 per cent of their Gross National Product (GNP) to ODA, and within that target, to earmark 0.15 percent to 0.20 percent for the LDCs. We also urge that the provision of official aid should respect the national development priorities of developing countries, and that conditions attached to ODA should be brought to an end.
- 'We advocate a solution for the serious global, regional and local environmental problems facing humanity, based on the recognition of the North's ecological debt and the principle of common but differentiated responsibilities of developed and developing countries.'

Group of 77 South Summit, Havana, 10–14 April 2000.

Discussions tend to polarise when they take a North–South dimension. Grievances from other, related and unrelated, international negotiations spill over into those on climate change. This is inevitable, since many key North–South issues remain unaddressed for years, and since the climate change negotiations ran parallel to the UNCED negotiations (Chatterjee and Finger 1994: 40; Arnold 1993; Nath 1993; Goldemberg 1994). More than 150 interviews with negotiators and stakeholders in the developing world indicate that the South increasingly saw climate change as yet another North–South issue. This led to renewed demands for the establishment of a new order corresponding to the 1960s demands for the New International Economic Order (NIEO) and for principles that would guarantee the right of the developing countries to grow, to combat poverty and equitably to share global environmental resources.

The North–South polarisation caused the climate change issue to be linked with inequities in the international economic order, for example in relation to the textile trade within the WTO, to intellectual property rights in relation to the Biodiversity Convention (Chatterjee and Finger 1994: 42), to the timber trade, to the falling price of raw materials, and so on. However, unlike in some of these other issues, where the developing countries felt that they had to appeal to the good nature and the moral values of the North, in the case of climate change they felt that they had a strong case, since the North was clearly the 'bad guy' polluting the global atmosphere. Righteous indignation gave way to legal positioning, and linkages were made with other issues, because climate change 'gave new leverage to their claims for a better redistribution of wealth among nations' (Goldemberg 1994: 177).

The changing political situation in the post-Cold War period, where the Eastern Bloc, instead of being an alternative source of funding and assistance, was itself competing for scarce help from the developed countries, has also increased the vulnerability of developing countries. The latter were increasingly convinced that this new role of the former Eastern Bloc countries would increase the inequalities in power between North and South. Third World intellectuals felt they confronted a world characterised by just one dominant economic ideology and by overwhelming US military power, where a handful of very rich countries was trying to monopolise military, medical and energy technology, and hemming in the rest of the world with restrictions and conditionalities (Rao 1993: 319; Arnold 1993; Rao 1994: 399; Agarwal et al. 1992: 12; Nyerere et *al.* 1990). The developed countries were seen to set the global agenda and to manoeuvre issues to fora that supported their interests. As examples, developing country experts cite Northern neglect of developmental issues at UNCED, the disappearance of the NIEO from international discussions, and the movement of the intellectual property rights discussion from the World Intellectual Property Organisation to the WTO.

To the extent that developing countries were able to negotiate certain elements that favoured them, such as in the Law of the Sea, the Biodiversity Convention, and the Toxic Waste Convention, there was a feeling that the US would then protect its own interests by not ratifying the agreements. The US withdrawal from Kyoto is seen as another such move, very much in line with previous US practice in international environmental conventions.

Experience of past international negotiations leads developing countries to see new Northern moves and initiatives with mistrust, as neo-colonialist. The South expects the inequitable economic order to be complemented by an inequitable environmental order; the two are seen as intimately linked. Only if the economic order is changed, raw materials priced fairly, import restrictions in developed countries removed, and debt cancelled will the South have the opportunity to increase its revenues and be able to invest in environmental protection and modern technologies.

All this means that the South tends to prepare positions demanding financial assistance and compensation and technology transfer at non-commercial rates, and these positions are used in a wide range of negotiations, irrespective of the precise nature of the subject matter. The South appears unable to refine its negotiating position and go beyond rhetorical statements of Third World solidarity. This posturing can be dealt with easily by the developed countries because, on the one hand, the developing countries would like to be like the West and, on the other hand, they reject Western rationality; they feel that 'whining' does not help and one takes what one can get, yet they would like to see themselves as 'poor and noble ... avenging historical wrongs' (as an interviewee put it); they want to stand up to the West, but are afraid of retaliation.

NORTHERN COALITIONS

The North, for the purpose of the climate change negotiations, comprises forty countries plus the European Union. The dominant group is the EU, consisting of 15 countries, but it is likely to grow to include new candidate members from Central and Eastern Europe. EU policy is closely coordinated, and in the case of climate change, it is the Council of Ministers that takes decisions regarding its negotiating mandate.

The US is one of the most influential members of the Northern coalition, by virtue of its population, size of economy and the volume of emissions. Its willingness to go it alone also makes it a force to be reckoned with in the negotiations. Nevertheless, Japan, the US, Switzerland, Canada, Norway and New Zealand have formed a group with the acronym JUSSCANNZ. This is a strange coalition when one considers that in the early 1990s Canada and Norway aspired to pioneer environmental responsibility, and Japan, as host, supports the Kyoto Protocol. But over time, clear similarities between these countries have emerged. These include converging views on sinks, reluctance to make binding commitments, and strong emphasis on the need for market mechanisms. The Bonn 2001 negotiations, however, reveal that these countries can at times withdraw their support for the US position.

Within Eastern and Central Europe, Belarus, although in Annex I of the Convention, is not included in Annex B of the Protocol and is, like Turkey, in limbo in the negotiations. The Central Group–11, established in 2000, comprises Bulgaria, the Czech Republic, Slovakia, Estonia, Hungary, Latvia, Lithuania, Poland, Romania, Croatia and Slovenia. These countries have relatively low incomes, small economies, struggling political systems and aspirations to EU membership. Russia and Ukraine, both fairly large economies, seek to have an independent identity in the process.

Russia and Ukraine have also joined an Umbrella Group with Japan, Iceland, USA, Canada, Australia, Norway and New Zealand. This group was formed to see if they could develop a common position regarding some of the flexibility mechanisms, in particular emissions trading.

Liechtenstein and Monaco sought admission to Annex I by an amendment, and are in no particular coalition.

THE EUROPEAN UNION

The EU has been actively involved in the climate change negotiations. In 1990, in response to the growing evidence of the problem, the Council of Environment Ministers adopted a common target to stabilise the CO_2 emissions of the 12 member states at 1990 levels by the year 2000. During that period many member states were actively seeking or had adopted domestic targets in relation to one or more greenhouse gases (see Table 8). In principle, the Europeans agreed to some burden sharing, allowing less developed European countries to increase their emissions. In the six years that followed, however, although there was considerable discussion, little progress was made in determining what the burden sharing agreement was actually going to look like (Wettestad 2000).

Meanwhile, efforts to develop a common EU carbon tax were initiated. The idea was that such a tax at EU level would help member states to reduce CO_2 emissions. This would not affect the relative competitiveness of energy-intensive industry within the EU. However, some countries, including the United Kingdom, were reluctant to hand authority over fiscal matters to the Commission; the process of negotiating a common tax continues (Dahl 2000; Gupta and Ringius 2001). In 1996, in anticipation of agreement in Kyoto, the Dutch government asked a research institute to develop a system of burden-sharing or target-sharing among EU member states. In response the institute prepared a proposal with targets based on three criteria (see Box 11). These targets were discussed and negotiated and the EU Council of Ministers decided to develop a negotiating position based on the acceptance of a common target of −15 per cent for 2010 in relation to three key gases, to be divided among member states. The range extended from a −25 per cent target for some countries to a +40 per cent target for others (see Table 8). This strengthened the EU negotiating position. By December 1997, the pressure on the rest of the developed countries had increased, and

TABLE 8   The evolution of EU emissions targets (%)

	Domestic goal, early 1990s[a][b]	Pre–Kyoto willingness (-15)[c]	Post–Kyoto willingness[d] (-8)[e]
Austria	Reduce CO_2 by 20% 2000/1988	−25	−13
Belgium	Reduce CO_2 by 5% 2000/1990	−10	−7.5
Denmark	Reduce CO_2 by 20% 2005/1988	−25	−21
Finland	Stabilise CO_2 2000/1990	−10	0
France	Stabilise per capita CO_2 at 2 tonnes by 2000	0	0
Germany	Reduce CO_2 by 25% 2000/1987	−25	−21
Greece	Support EU target	+30	+25
Ireland		+15	+13
Italy	Stabilise CO_2 2000/1990; reduce CO_2 by 20% 2005/1990	−7	−6.5
Luxembourg	Support EU target	−30	−28
Netherlands	Reduce CO_2 by 3–5% 2000/1990	−10	−6
Portugal	Support EU target	+40	+27
Spain		+17	+15
Sweden	Support EC/EFTA target	+5	+4
UK	Stabilise CO_2 emissions 2005/1990	−10	−12

[a] Compiled by Wolters, Swager and Gupta 1991.
[b] Common 1992 target: willingness to accept common stabilisation target for 2000/1990.
[c] Conclusions of the Council of Environment ministers in March 1997 in relation to three gases.
[d] Common Kyoto target: willingness to accept a common −8% target for 2008–12 for six gases in relation to 1990.
[e] Conclusions of the Council of Environment ministers in June 1998 in relation to six gases.

they agreed to a common target of −5.2 per cent in the budget period 2008–12; after considerable bargaining the EU accepted the common target of −8 per cent in relation to the base year 1990. Within the EU, a burden-sharing agreement was reached in March 1998, ranging from −28 per cent to +27 per cent.

Efforts to ratify the Protocol were slowed down because of US reluctance to pursue ratification. The literature promoted ratification by the EU (Grubb *et al.* 1999; Gupta and Grubb 2000; Oberthür and Ott 1999), which intensified efforts to promote ratification and entry into force by 2002. President Bush's reluctance to go further with the Kyoto Protocol has intensified the efforts within the Union, and the Swedish Presidency of the EU announced recently that the EU and the US have agreed to disagree, and that EU countries will try to complete ratification procedures by the end of 2001.

EASTERN AND CENTRAL EUROPE

The Eastern Bloc countries were relatively powerful in the early 1980s. By the end of the decade the Berlin Wall had collapsed, and the USSR's control was decreasing. With the call for independence by the Baltic states, and perestroika, the USSR began to split up into a number of countries. With the death of Tito in Yugoslavia and the fall of Ceausescu in Romania, the former satellite states went through domestic political upheaval followed by reform. These events amounted to a major shock to the economy and infrastructure of these countries and most went into economic decline. Many aspired to EU membership. Some decided to take on the status and responsibilities of developed countries. Some collapsed completely and became unwittingly part of the developing world.

By 1992, Belarus, Czechoslovakia, Estonia, Hungary, Latvia, Lithuania, Poland, Romania the Russian Federation and Ukraine were willing to accept stabilisation targets if they were given some concessions regarding base years and the strictness of implementation. A few years later, Croatia and Slovenia joined this group. On the basis of a re-consideration of its national economy, Belarus withdrew. Czechoslovakia split into two countries, and both have accepted new targets.

By 1997, the political (rather than economic) diversity in these countries was reflected more clearly in the Kyoto Protocol. Bulgaria, the Czech Republic, Estonia, Latvia, Lithuania, Romania, Slovakia and Slovenia decided to go beyond stabilisation and accept a −8 per cent target. This may have reflected their aspiration to share the common EU target. Poland negotiated for −6 per cent, Croatia for −5 per cent; Ukraine and Russia settled for stabilisation.

Box 8 shows that, unlike the rest of eastern and central Europe, Russia and Ukraine were allowed to increase their GHG emissions to 1990 levels. These countries may not be allowed to increase their emissions in the future, but must rather stabilise or reduce them further; of course, they may be gambling on the possibility that they will be allowed to increase their emissions in the second budget period. But there is in effect a cap on the possible growth of these countries' economies, unless they can effectively find ways to decouple their economic growth from emissions. At the same time, by accepting these targets these countries are able to encash unused portions of their assigned amounts through emission trading with other developed countries. If we compare their situation with that of the developing countries, we can see that they are apparently less afraid to take on quantitative commitments and do not immediately fear potential caps on economic growth; they are rewarded for taking on such commitments through the possibility of emission trading.

DEVELOPING COUNTRY COALITIONS

The non-Annex I countries consist of about 130 members of the G77 and 23 non-G77 countries. The G77 has three regional groupings: Africa comprises 53 countries, the Latin American and Caribbean group has 32 countries, not including Mexico, and Asia has 36 countries. The status of Mexico is not entirely certain since it is a member of the OECD and is thus excluded from G77. However, in the climate change negotiations, Mexico has avoided inclusion in the list of the developed countries. There is also a more informal group, called GRILA, which comprises 16 like-minded countries within

---

Box 13   Special provisions for OPEC countries

The climate convention and the Kyoto Protocol make special provisions for countries dependent on oil exports. Article 4.10 of the FCCC states: 'The Parties shall, in accordance with Article 10, take into consideration in the implementation of the commitments of the Convention the situation of Parties, particularly developing country Parties, with economies that are vulnerable to the adverse effects of the implementation of measures to respond to climate change. This applies notably to Parties with economies that are highly dependent on income generated from the production, processing and export, and/or consumption of fossil fuels and associated energy-intensive products and/or the use of fossil fuels for which such Parties have serious difficulties in switching to alternatives'.

At the sixth Conference of the Parties in Bonn 2001, special attention was paid to the concerns of these countries including a decision to help these countries strengthen their capacity to improve their efficiency in the fossil-fuel industry and to help them diversify their economy.

---

the Latin American group. The Latin American and Caribbean group is fairly active in the negotiations. Asia consists of 45 countries, of which 9 are not in the G77. ASEAN countries and the League of Arab States have also been forming small regional networks to negotiate their several national interests.

Africa, with an annual per capita income of less than US$300, contributing 2–3 per cent of global GHG emissions (most of which come from South Africa), is at the losing end of climate change discussions. While it has the smallest volume of emissions, it is also the most vulnerable because it lacks both economic and technological capacity, and good governance systems that can respond effectively and fast to a crisis. The floods in Mozambique devastated the land, but the government was unable to respond in time. Other parts of Africa are ravaged by drought and disease. At the same time, there are limited efforts being made in African countries to try and deal with climate change.

Apart from the regional groupings there are issue-based coalitions. A dominant member within this group is OPEC, with 11 countries. The OPEC countries, with their considerable wealth, have sought a leadership role within the G77, especially when it was arguing in favour of the new international economic order. OPEC is also a generous donor, and influential in G77. OPEC countries tend to argue against binding commitments for developed countries, and to slow down the negotiations.

At the other end of the spectrum is the Alliance of Small Island States (AOSIS). This group has come together because of the climate-related vulnerability of its 42 countries, mostly small islands but also some small coastal states. In the early 1990s, AOSIS made an appeal: 'For us, the precautionary principle is much more than a semantic or theoretical exercise. It is an ecological and moral imperative. We do not have the luxury of waiting for conclusive proof as some have suggested in the past. The proof we fear will kill us' (cited in Wolters *et al*. 1991). Four members of this group are not independent states. The AOSIS countries have consistently pushed for tough targets and against loopholes in the Convention.

CURIOUS COALITIONS

There have on occasion been cross-cutting coalitions between Northern and Southern countries. Thus for example, there is a sort of coalition between Argentina, Kazakhstan and the Annex B countries in that the former two have stated their willingness to take on legally binding targets. There is an Environmental Integrity Group that consists of Mexico, South Korea and Switzerland, a motley combination of countries. In relation to JI/AIJ/CDM, there is a group of Southern countries that have always favoured the issue and have concurred with the developed country position on this. Since Bonn 2001, there appears to be a global coalition of countries minus the US.

A closer examination of the developed countries in terms of per capita income and per capita CO_2 emissions from industrial sources indicates that Norway, Iceland and Australia, very high on both counts, are allowed to increase their emissions. On the other hand,

Luxembourg, also very high, has made a commitment to reduce its emissions by 28 per cent, along with middle income countries such as Russia, Ukraine and Romania.

Within OPEC, per capita GNP varies from well under US$1000 (Nigeria) to more than US$22,000 (Qatar). Per capita CO_2 emissions also vary from about 1 tonne (Nigeria) to more than 28 tonnes (Qatar). There are five fairly poor countries (Algeria, Indonesia, Iran, Iraq, and Nigeria) and five fairly rich countries (Kuwait, Libya, Qatar, Saudi Arabia and United Arab Emirates) in this group.

The bulk of the small island states have relatively low emissions and national income. However, in this group Singapore stands out as an extremely rich country with fairly high emissions, Palau and Trinidad & Tobago are fairly rich countries with high emissions who have, apart from their island status, little in common with the other countries.

In Asia, per capita income varies hugely from Nepal (US$220) to Singapore (US$29,610); Israel, Brunei, Bahrain, South Korea, Taiwan and even Thailand are fairly rich. The rest of Asia is quite similar in per capita incomes and industrial CO_2 emissions.

Of the 53 African countries, 30 are least developed countries (LLDCs) with low incomes; only two African countries (Libya and the Seychelles) have a per capita income above US$3000. While Libya and South Africa's per capita emissions are very high, those of the Seychelles are considerably lower. Apart from these countries, there is considerable homogeneity.

Latin America, too, has some of the richest countries (Bahamas, Argentina, Barbados, Antigua & Barbuda, St Kitts & Nevis, Chile, Mexico and Trinidad & Tobago) and some of the poorest (Haiti and Nicaragua). Per capita CO_2 emissions are highest in Trinidad & Tobago.

If one were to take a fresh look at the world on the basis of per capita incomes, it would immediately become obvious that the distinction North (Annex I) and South (Non-Annex I) is losing relevance. Singapore could easily be classified among the richest countries in the world. The Bahamas, Brunei, Israel, Kuwait, and Qatar are as rich as Spain and Portugal. On the other hand, Ukraine, Russia and the Central Group–11 countries are as poor as the bulk of middle-income countries. The blurred distinctions between rich and poor make it all the more difficult for existing alliances to maintain the credibility of their positions.

We are witnessing a change in the dimensions of the North–South debate. It is not so much a debate between the rich and the poor, as between those who want to belong to the club of rich countries and those who recognise that they can only belong to the club of the poor.

WHAT FOLLOWS?

The deep rifts that traditionally divide the North from the South on a number of issues have been imported into the climate change arena.

The climate change issue, because of its far-reaching consequences, has brought some of the smallest and most remote nations of the world to the centre of the debate, complicating earlier North–South negotiations. In addition, the end of the Cold War has led to new alliances based more on geographical proximity and self-image than on economic and political similarity, and this too has complicated North–South relations.

There are legitimate issues nevertheless that concern poor and rich countries alike; but the legitimacy of their classification into one or other category is fast being undermined by the lack of clear criteria. This has led to the adoption of new reasons for Northern countries to justify the claim that countries in the South need to 'graduate' into the North for the purpose of the climate negotiations. Although there is much talk on this issue, it is also clear that only 7 of the 153 developing countries fall into the category of rich or very rich countries – a marginal number. In the process people are forgetting that at least thirteen of the forty so-called 'developed' countries are in fact only middle-income countries in the midst of political and economic crises – they do not really qualify as rich countries, but are being allowed into the club at a price. No wonder that Belarus has rethought its position and withdrawn from the club of rich nations.

CHAPTER 7

THE NON-STATE ACTORS AND COALITIONS

THE GROWING MASS OF NON-STATE ACTORS

The climate change issue affects all of us, but the negotiations are limited to states and their representatives. However, non-state actors are invited to participate as observers in the international process. This is allowed by Article 71 of the United Nations Charter (1945) and was reaffirmed by a decision at UNCED in 1992. The increasing numbers of non-state actors participating in the negotiations and in associated side-events are in many ways increasing the influence of the process, but they also cramp the negotiations. These actors include environmental groups, faith-based organisations, development organisations, and last but certainly not least, the industrial sector. At the first negotiating session in Chantilly in 1991 more than fifty NGOs were present. By the first Conference of the Parties, 165 NGOs, 12 intergovernmental organisations and 19 UN agencies were present. By the third Conference the numbers had increased to 236 NGOs, 15 intergovernmental organisations and 27 UN agencies. Press coverage puts the key issues before the general public. Non-state actors play an influential role in the domestic context in some countries. This chapter briefly highlights the nature of the discussions and the issues involved. At the international level, the non-state actors can essentially be divided into three groups with somewhat contradictory goals: the environmental NGOs (ENGOs), industry, and the research community. The presence of these groups leads to 10,000 people or more participating in the negotiations.

ENVIRONMENTAL NGOS

Since the 1980s, environmental NGOs have realised that they can optimise their influence on the international negotiating process by developing common positions and by pooling resources. Hence in 1989, the environmental NGOs established themselves as the Climate Action Network, and over the years have added about 300 members to their list. The Climate Action Network has eight regional chapters.

BOX 14 Reading material provided by environmental NGOs

Although many have a lighter side to them, the publications of the environmental NGOs have become increasingly complex and sophisticated over the years, but they still make for easier reading than the voluminous material provided by scientists. The NGO publications include:

- *Earth Negotiations Bulletin* A factual account of the daily negotiations produced by the International Institute for Sustainable Development.
- *ENB – On the Side* A factual account of the daily side-events that take place at the negotiations, published by the International Institute for Sustainable Development and the FCCC secretariat.
- *ECO* A humorous daily account of important negotiations produced by Non-Governmental Environmental Groups since the Stockholm Environment Conference in 1972. The ECO on the Climate Negotiations are produced by the Climate Action Network Groups.
- *Clime Asia* Issues of regional interest to South Asia produced by Climate Action Network South Asia.
- *IMPACT* Issues of regional interest to Africa produced by Climate Network Africa.
- *Hotspot* Issues of regional interest to Europe by Climate Network Europe.
- *Climate Notes* Issues of interest on climate change explained in detail by the World Resources Institute.

Sometimes the interests and needs of individual NGOs diverge from the group, as reflected in the range of journals and papers that are distributed internationally.

Many ENGOs have their own distinct profiles and positions. The World Wide Fund for Nature, Greenpeace International, Friends of

---

Box 15   Make or break Kyoto

In 2000, the World Wide Fund for Nature produced a document in which they listed the features of a successful protocol and those of an unsuccessful protocol. According to them, the Kyoto Protocol can be successful if:

- targets are met through domestic action;
- targets are met through emission reduction and not through sinks;
- the CDM prioritises clean and positive list technologies, i.e. technologies that focus on energy efficiency and renewables;
- if there is strong enforcement.

On the other hand, they argue that the Protocol may fail if:

- countries can buy hot air;
- sinks can be used to fulfil targets;
- CDM is used to promote nuclear, large hydro and clean coal;
- native forests are cleared to make way for high CO_2-absorbing plantations;
- countries are allowed to borrow from the future to meet their targets.

At the same time, Agarwal (2000), of the Centre for Science and Environment in New Delhi, writes that the environmentally conscious want the Protocol to be ecologically effective; the poor want it to be equitable and socially just; and the rest want it to be economically effective. He argues that for ecologically effective action, stabilisation should be at 450 ppmv (parts per million by volume), and that eventually the North will have to reduce emissions by 90 per cent and the South by 50 per cent. For climate agreement to be economically effective, the developed countries will need flexible mechanisms. For it to be equitable, it is necessary that they promote zero emission technologies, so that over time the discussion over emission entitlements becomes irrelevant as the whole world switches to renewables.

Although there are differences in nuance, both groups in effect argue in favour of promoting renewables through flexibility mechanisms.

Sources: WWF 2000; Agarwal 2000.

the Earth, among the international NGOs actively engaged in the field, produce a wide range of literature and use a number of strategies to influence the process of negotiation. There are also organisations that provide scientific information on environmental issues, and sometimes lobby with other groups. Major Southern NGOs include the South Centre in Geneva, the Centre for Science and Environment in New Delhi, the Bangladesh Centre for Advanced Studies in Dhaka, Pelangi in Jakarta, and Earthlife Africa in Johannesburg. The World Resources Institute in Washington, the Royal Institute of International Affairs and the Foundation for International Environmental Law and Development in London, the Center for the Sustainable Development of the Americas in Washington, the International Institute for Sustainable Development in Canada, the Wuppertal Institute in Germany, and the Institute for Environmental Studies in Amsterdam also provide scientific material to support negotiations. In the domestic context, many NGOs produce their own journals and cover climate change issues in them (see Box 14).

The ENGOs have been coordinating their position over the years, and although many were critical of the Kyoto Protocol, they still see it as a vital first step in a long and arduous process. Many came up with positions to discuss ways to increase the environmental integrity of the Protocol (see Box 15).

At the same time, ENGOs do not always agree on issues. While some believe that allowing sinks in the implementation of the Protocol is unwise, others argue the opposite (see Box 16).

As mentioned before, there is a conflict between the Northern, primarily environmental, NGOs and the Southern, primarily developmental, NGOs on the definition of the issues. 'While the former argue the need for curbs to be placed on economic growth, the latter argue that the worst problems are created by industry and over-consumption in the North and by inequalities in the global economic system' (McCormick 1999: 60). There is a difference of opinion between those NGOs who would like to close the loopholes and those who would like to be innovative in the process of identifying solutions to keep countries on board.

BOX 16   'Sinking the Kyoto Protocol?'

A group of ENGOs – Earthlife Africa Johannesburg, Environmental Monitoring Group, Group for Environmental Monitoring, Greater Edendale Environmental Network, South African Climate Action Network – recently published a paper on the inclusion of sinks in the implementation of the Protocol. The theoretical assumption that countries can compensate for emissions by promoting sinks is based, in their view, on the naive notion that the climate system is linear, instead of dynamic and unpredictable. Furthermore, allowing such forestry projects delays the pressure to reduce the use of fossil fuels and makes reduction more challenging in the future. In developing sinks, countries will be motivated to use trees that absorb the most carbon; this will inevitably lead to plantations at the cost of biodiversity, conservation, and genetic diversity. They make a strong case for excluding land-use change and forestry in the first commitment period. Their reasons include: that the scientific uncertainty about how to measure sinks could undermine real emission reductions; the questionable permanence of any given form of land use; tree plantations, as opposed to naturally occurring forest cover, are not ecologically effective, and lead to marginalisation of forest dwellers and subsistence communities; the notion of forests as sinks does not take into account potential impacts of climate change on existing forests and agriculture worldwide; and, finally, that it may undermine other multilateral agreements on bio-diversity, wetlands, desertification and forests. They are also afraid that by extending the definition of sinks, developed countries could claim that they need take no action to reduce their emissions, and this would undermine the effectiveness of the climate change treaty.

At the same time, there are NGOs in Latin America who believe that sinks can benefit local communities and rural livelihoods: if sinks are prepared on waste lands, provide new jobs, take the social and cultural context into account, and do not lead to loss of biodiversity, then the inclusion of sinks may also address a number of related issues as well as climate change. This would be a win–win situation.

However, many ENGOs are afraid that, since resources are limited and cost-effectiveness is a goal with the investors, cost-effectiveness will be achieved at the cost of biodiversity and local cultures, and may lead to forest plantations that replace either quality agricultural land or existing forest land, in which case carbon sinks will be enhanced at the cost of local sustainability. Developing rules that can promote sinks without compromising on local sustainability is the challenge. For many it is highly controversial whether this is possible within the context of a market-based instrument.

Source: EAJ *et al.* 2000; http://www.gn.apc.org.

INDUSTRY AND BUSINESS: 'RUSSIAN ROULETTE' OR 'CASINO CAPITALISM'

The climate change issue is so closely connected with economic profits and the survival of industry that it is inevitable that business and industry have taken a key interest in the process since the beginning of the negotiations, at both the domestic and the international levels. In the world of market mechanisms, the survival of the fittest is the rule. The question is: the fittest for what?

The initial reaction of industry was to oppose the process of climate policy-making by claiming that the science was inadequate. The Global Climate Coalition was one such group. It was established in 1989 and its choice of name can confuse the outsider about its purpose. It includes about 60 companies and corporations that are not yet convinced of the climate change science. They have been known to argue that climate policy could be like Russian roulette, as countries and industries take on commitments that may have fatal consequences for their own economic stability (Stone 1999). They were joined over the years by the Coalition for Vehicle Choice (and its Global Climate Information project), the Climate Council (a lobby group which, *inter alia*, supports OPEC countries with arguments and represents interests similar to OPEC countries) and CEFIC, the federation of chemical industries which opposes climate measures (CEO 2000: 38). The Carbon Club was instrumental in pushing for the Byrd–Hagel Resolution (see Box 5) and launched a US$13 million campaign to state that developing countries had no commitments under the Protocol and that its implementation would cost the US a lot of money. At the same time, the Carbon Club was reportedly trying to convince the developing countries that they could not afford to undertake emission limitations themselves. Thus Exxon Corporation reportedly stated at a meeting in China that developing countries should work with these companies to resist policies that could strangle economic growth (Oberthür and Ott 1999: 73).

At the same time, some industries have discovered the potential of developing new businesses. This led some to break away from the Global Climate Coalition and to present themselves as relatively 'green'. Some of these are truly interested in promoting their technologies, while others are hedging their bets. Some are becoming emission brokers, who help to bring capital and environmental markets together. This process is referred to as casino capitalism (CEO 2000: 14).

The European Round Table (ERT) of industrialists includes 48 captains of industry from the largest and most influential transnational corporations, and has a working group on climate change that is trying to come up with measures that will make regulation unnecessary. UNICE, an employers' federation in Europe, is lobbying hard for voluntary action from industry and participation in the flexible mechanisms. The International Chamber of Commerce presents a vision of industry that is willing to cooperate and take action. However, as Vice-President McCormick warns: 'If, instead, they [governments] choose a "quick-fix, look-good" deal that causes a dramatic and costly shift in the way industrialised countries use energy, they will risk undermining our global and national economies. And they will jeopardise the environment as well' (McCormick 2000).

The oil industry is a major source of emissions. Exxon Mobil and Texaco have relatively conservative positions, arguing in favour of more science; Shell and BP Amoco are investing increasingly in renewables and in public awareness campaigns. Texaco has left the Global Climate Coalition. Shell and BP Amoco have published advertisements and made statements about how they are now energy services companies and no longer oil companies. They are making efforts to convey the message that they are increasingly greening their production processes and investing in renewable energy. Shell, for example, has announced that it will reduce its emissions by 10 per cent from 1990 levels by 2002. At the same time sceptics argue that this is all 'greenwash', that by spending some money on renewables and advertisements the companies are hoping to divert interest from their huge core businesses, which are increasing oil production every year. They even report that while these two companies are ostensibly presenting themselves as green companies they are also members of the American Petroleum Institute, a climate change sceptic, and the Business Round Table, which opposes measures, and that BP Amoco has made contributions to US Congress members who oppose environmental policies and ratification of Kyoto (CEO 2000: 31).

The chemical industry produces large quantities of emissions and HFCs. Some of these companies are taking a proactive stance. Thus Claude Fussler (1998) of Dow Europe has been developing a theoretical and management approach to climate change. He encourages business to focus on eco-efficiency (producing more from less), creating value for customers, having clear objectives and targets for sustainability, empowering employees, citizens and communities, caring about ethics and socio-economic security, thinking creatively and encouraging dialogue with the forces that are trying to reshape the world. Some companies such as DuPont, Bayer and ICI claim to have reduced their greenhouse gases by 30–60 per cent simply by including CFCs and N_2O that were being phased out for other reasons. Many of these companies have adopted some energy efficiency targets. DuPont also has a target to increase its use of renewable energy to 10 per cent (Van der Woerd et al. 2000). Holliday, Chairman and CEO of DuPont, states: 'At DuPont we are preparing our company for what we see as a long journey to a more climate-friendly and environmentally sound global economy. While we have already reduced our global greenhouse gases by nearly 60 per cent, we have committed to take the next leap forward, setting new goals for 2010; reducing global carbon-equivalent greenhouse gas emissions by 65 per cent, using 1990 as a base year; and using renewable resources for 10 per cent of our global energy use' (Pew Centre/ IHT 2000).

In the automobile industry, some slow progress is being made. In July 1999, a voluntary agreement was developed between the EU and the automobile industry that sells in Europe to reduce average carbon emissions by 140 g/km by 2008, which amounts to a 25 per cent reduction. This would in effect lead to a new generation of lightweight cars that could run on diesel or fuel cells. In the US, efforts were made to develop a Partnership for a New Generation of Vehicles (PNGV) to promote cars that did not sacrifice the attributes that people want from cars, but did try and work on emissions. This programme, partly subsidised by the US government, has looked at lightweight materials, alternative fuels and hybrid cars. After Kyoto, Ford has begun to invest in fuel cell research, hybrid sport utility vehicles and electric cars. General Motors and Toyota are also collaborating on new research. General Motors is cooperating with BP, and Ford with BP and Mobil, to identify alternative fuels. Taguchi, President of Toyota, claims proudly: 'Toyota created the world's first mass-produced hybrid electric vehicle, the Prius, as one of several diverse approaches to a cleaner car, cleaner air, and a cleaner environment' (Pew Centre/IHT 2000).

The Pew Centre on Global Climate Change, with members including United Technologies, Intel, AEP, DuPont, BP, Shell, Toyota, Boeing, ABB, Lockheed Martin, Enron, Edison International, established in 1998, aims at 'safe climate and sound business'. They too focus on promoting voluntary action as a way to deal with climate change. They published an advertisement in the *International Herald Tribune* stating: 'Think industry isn't concerned about climate change? Think again. More and more business leaders agree something must be done. They are not just talking. They're taking responsibility. Investing in Answers. Showing what works...'

The World Business Council for Sustainable Development (WBCSD) states that it is committed to sustainable development. Membership of this Council is by invitation only: 'The WBCSD provides leadership as a catalyst for change toward sustainable development; it promotes eco-efficiency, innovation and responsible entrepreneurship. It also cooperates with governments, non-governmental organisations and other groups to bring about solutions'. The European Business Council for a Sustainable Energy Future (E5) was established in 1996 and includes the cogeneration industry (combined heating/cooling and power generation) among its members. The insurance industry is also becoming increasingly active and alert as a result of the increasing number of incidents. The insurance company Munich Re prepared a note in 1998 to show the increase in storms, hurricanes and floods over the last forty years and the impact on costs. While they are actively trying to show the increase in the number of extreme weather events and associated costs, their motive may be that they can then increase premiums.

There is also a very strong nuclear lobby at the meetings. The European Atomic Forum, the European Nuclear Society and the International Nuclear Forum are just some of the groups lobbying for a nuclear comeback.

There are clearly industries that oppose the climate change process and challenge the science; these industries have found a major supporter in the White House. At the same time, many of the other big players are portraying themselves as the people with the answers. What binds this group together is their demand for clear guidelines and flexibility to allow the market mechanism to function in a simple and straightforward manner. They do not want to be overburdened with a large number of cumbersome rules and red tape. As Moorcroft of the WBCSD puts it: 'If the policy-makers can get the framework conditions right, and if business continues to show vision and leadership, there is no doubt that a sense of progress will emerge. And perhaps that will alleviate some of the anxiety we all feel about the climate change problem' (Moorcroft 2000).

Most Western governments are increasingly enthusiastic about the role of industry in the climate change discussions. They believe that if they can send out signals that industry is willing to pick up, then there is an incentive for industry to develop low or zero GHG technologies, and this will lead to the diffusion of such technologies worldwide, ultimately addressing the climate change problem.

Sceptics argue that industry is just trying to pre-empt the negotiation process. The International Emissions Trading Association includes Shell, BP Amoco, Statoil, Tokyo Electric Power, the Australian Stock Exchange and the International Petroleum Exchange, and they want to develop a market even if the Protocol never enters into effect. Many are afraid that these companies wish to set the rules in advance of the democratic process in the negotiations and that given their size and influence they may well be able to do so. Others are afraid of the potential for black markets in credits and credit laundering. Some argue that the corporate sector has merely pseudo solutions to offer. The Corporate Europe Observatory is extremely sceptical about the role of industry, seeing it as taking over the climate agenda: 'The net effect of corporate involvement, however, will be a corrupted and anaemic Kyoto Protocol. Corporations – efficiently organised in a complex web of national, regional and global groupings – have engaged in proactive lobbying to prevent what they consider to be the worst case scenario – binding government regulations to force businesses to reduce greenhouse gas emissions' (CEO 2000). It argues that industry has put multiple market mechanisms on the agenda to increase its own negotiating room.

OTHER SOCIAL ACTORS

While climate researchers have been focusing on climate related issues longer, other disciplines have become involved since the 1990s: economists, lawyers, social scientists and ecologists have delved rapidly into the scientific research. That research is being collated through the Intergovernmental Panel on Climate Change (see Chapter 2). Several universities and institutes are engaged in it, and these researchers are increasingly present at negotiations as observers, with their latest publications and journals and sometimes even easy-to-understand posters. They also hold side-events to communicate scientific information to the negotiators in easily digestible format. At the same time there are international networks trying to provide information on key issues, for example, the Climate Change Knowledge Network of 14 organisations representing different regions of the world.

A number of intergovernmental organisations also participate actively in the negotiations. These include the United Nations Environment Programme, United Nations Development Programme, International Civil Aviation Organisation, United Nations Conference on Trade and Development, the World Bank, the World Meteorological Organisation, the International Standards Organisation and many others. The International Coalition of Local Environmental Initiatives represents 240 cities in Europe and North America. Even politicians seem to have entered the international fray with their own agenda. Globe International comprises 550 parliamentarians from over 100 countries. This group believes in the need to promote policy-making in the environmental field, and states that 'the obligation is on us parliamentarians to keep the process alive, and ensure that it remains linked to the electorates around the world, rather than cut off in the corridors, couched in the language of economists and bankers ... we shall work for the rapid ratification of the Kyoto Protocol, which ... offers opportunities for both industry and the creation of jobs' (Globe International Press Release, 14 November 1998).

KEY ISSUES OF CONCERN

There are major conflicts of interests within and between the three groups mentioned above. Within industry, there is a conflict between the large and the small. The large industries are able to influence the process; the small are influenced by the process. In many ways the large bodies stand to gain at the cost of the small because they have more resources and can, if necessary, adapt to changing circumstances. Within large companies there is conflict between diverging policies, and they often join different coalitions to keep all options open. But industry can both have the answers and be the cause of the problems. Thus they can develop the technologies and move towards sustainable development. At the same time, if the pressure is taken off, they are inclined to promote the technologies that cause the problem. To that extent they are absolutely essential to the negotiating process. A major problem is that Southern business is absent from the negotiations; this impedes understanding of the problems in importing the older technologies, the criteria for importing new technologies, and the long-term implications for their survival.

Furthermore, there is conflict between business and ENGOs; the latter want to ensure environmental integrity and to push for a foolproof system of emission reductions in order to deal with the environmental problems. For most of industry, the struggle is to keep the system free of binding commitments that restrict its freedom to manoeuvre in the international market. The information provided by the different social actors varies. While ENGOs such as WWF distribute T-shirts saying 'save the climate – that's my job', and the National Resource Defence Council points out that large numbers of new jobs are possible through environmental policy, others, such as the Global Climate Coalition, focus on potential job losses. Clearly there will be losers and winners; but whether there will be net gain for society appears to be anybody's guess. Not even the most sophisticated scenario developers can provide more than an educated guess about what may happen in volatile markets and under a changing climate whose impacts may be felt anywhere in the world (see the IPCC report, Nakićenović *et al.* 2000). At the same time, there is a new trend of coalitions – Greenpeace has developed an initiative with Shell in relation to solar energy. The WWF has launched the Climate Savers Programme (www.wwf.org/climatesavers); the Environment Defense Fund in the US has established the Partnership for Climate Action and collaborates with BP, Shell, DuPont and others (www.environmentaldefense.org).

Within the social NGOs there are those who wish to keep the development agenda alive, and those who wish to focus single-mindedly on environmental issues. There are two elements to this debate. At the philosophical level, the issue is how to define development. Is development aping the West and buying into the ideological underpinnings of the modern, market-oriented liberal society? These issues have been highlighted in a number of works (McCormick 1999: 58; Chatterjee and Finger 1994). Northern environmental groups tend to focus on environmental protection, believing that society is rich enough to take measures. Southern groups focus on patterns of over-consumption and global inequalities. At a less philosophical level, the debate is simply about who can develop and when. The development organisations are fighting for the right to develop, and want developing countries to adopt available appropriate technologies to push the process of development. Environmental groups are applying the brakes, arguing that many of these technologies are inappropriate from an environmental perspective and that developing countries should adopt a short-cut to development. The problem with the short-cut is the bill.

Within the environmental NGOs too there is a key challenge. This is the challenge of trying, on the one hand, to develop a common position with other environmental groups and, on the other hand, to represent the views of their domestic constituencies. This is,

BOX 17   Mixed signals

Are developing countries receiving mixed signals? On the one hand they are being told to liberalise: liberalisation will address their economic problems and help them to become rich. On the other hand they are being accused, at least by the US administration, of not doing enough to curb their emissions. Does liberalisation go hand in hand with emission reduction?

Climate change negotiations aim at promoting the transfer of technologies that reduce emissions; meanwhile, developed countries have been promoting the transfer of technologies that in fact lead to increased emissions. Most developed countries have, for example, export credit agencies. These agencies use tax money to promote exports to developing countries. In the period 1994–99 these agencies provided US\$44 billion in loans, equity contributions, guarantees or investment insurance to leverage another US\$60 billion to promote projects like fossil-fuel power plants, oil and gas resource use, and energy intensive manufacturing in the developing countries. Only US\$2 billion were used to promote renewable energy. At the same time the financial mechanisms under the climate agreements are supposed to promote environmentally friendly technologies!

Source: Maurer 2000.

of course, similar to the 'three level game' that takes place within the EU, where individual countries have to come to a common position while still representing national interests; and then they have to go and find a common position with the rest of the world while still representing EU and national interests. However, while the EU has developed a relatively sophisticated mechanism to deal with this, the environmental groups are still in the process of balancing the three levels of negotiation.

From a North–South perspective, the climate change discussions may force the issue of leapfrog technology transfer. If that happens, it may well be the case that we are able to address the climate change issue, but the implications for technological (and, hence, financial) dependence for developing countries may be serious. On the other hand, it may just be that the South gets mixed signals from the North; that there is normal technology transfer through the normal channels of foreign investment, and leapfrog technology transfer via the mechanisms under the Convention and Protocol. The environment may then lose out in favour of profits for industry and those who benefit from them (see Box 17).

While NGOs have traditionally opposed the agendas of governments, they are now even representing governments at the negotiating table. D. Pearlman of the Climate Council sat with OPEC negotiators to help them develop their positions. Lawyers from the Foundation of International Environmental Law and Development wore the country badges of some small island countries and helped them develop national and coalition positions at the negotiations. At the same time some industries have ensured that their positions have been internalised by their economic affairs ministries.

CHAPTER 8

DUE PROCESS AND THE RULE OF LAW: TOWARDS DECREASING TRANSPARENCY

LEGITIMACY: THE GROWING CHALLENGE

International law, unlike domestic law, survives on countries' good faith and good will. There is no international police to enforce international law. It becomes vital that international agreements be legitimate, that they follow the rule of law, have sound procedures, build on precedent and principle, and reflect the will of the negotiating countries; that there is some give and take in the process and that the agreements themselves set good precedents for the future. Only then will countries feel obliged to comply with the provisions of international law because of their long-term interest in having a stable and ostensibly fair global legal system.

But the key issue remains: how does one ensure legitimacy of the process? In the formal sense, the answer is clear. The adoption of rules of procedure which allow for transparent preparation and decision-making is a clear indicator of fairness (see Box 18). But these may not be sufficient to guarantee legitimacy.

The rules do not and perhaps cannot take into account the vast structural differences between countries, the appropriateness of the timing of meetings, and the disparities in information. These seriously influence the ability of a country to represent itself and to take part effectively in international negotiations.

BOX 18   The rules of procedure: theory

In every negotiation process between countries, it is vital to have rules of procedure. These rules are normally drafted by the secretariat on the basis of earlier rules drafted for other negotiations. Then the countries negotiating adopt these rules by consensus. Once the rules are adopted, they govern the process of negotiating.

These rules generally specify how and when the agenda for the meetings is to be prepared, who has influence on it, what the language of the meetings is (in the UN context all formal meetings are in the six UN official languages), how many meetings can be organised and what is the character of the different kinds of meetings, who can chair the meetings, who has the right of intervention, when voting can take place, what kind of voting rules need to be put into place, who pays for the meetings, etc. Knowing this information in advance helps countries prepare for the meeting and ensures a fair negotiating process.

DIFFERENCES BETWEEN COUNTRIES IN PREPARATION FOR NEGOTIATING SESSIONS

A key difference between the developed and the developing countries is the structural stability of the domestic political, economic and legal systems. In some countries, there is a clear ideology whose basic tenets are shared by the majority of the people. In others, the basic ideology is the key battleground between competing political parties, who struggle to define the basic tenets of such an ideology. How does this affect the negotiating process? Quite simply as follows. If a proposal is made to transfer responsibility with respect to the implementation of an agreement to the private sector, countries that have experience with the private sector, have faith in the market mechanism and implicitly believe that governments need to be down-sized, tend to be able to accept such proposals in terms of their philosophical underpinning. The negotiators from these countries then move on to negotiate the exact wording of such an article, fine-tuning the language to ensure that their national interests are duly covered in the text. Within the South, the ideological process has not entirely settled down, neither in countries that are obviously in transition, such as China and India, nor in countries like Israel and South Africa, and although Latin America appears to accept the market ideology, the domestic discussion is far from settled. Thus, negotiators from countries that are going through an ideological debate do not have an automatic reflex that can either lead to support or rejection of whatever is on the negotiating table. They tend to focus more on the fundamental premise underlying the agreement, rather than the wording of the text. Inevitably this makes reaction to new proposals difficult in an international context, and hampers negotiations.

When applying this idea to the different countries in the world, it is clear that the OECD countries have a clear ideological common ground, although there may be shades of difference. The former members of the Eastern Bloc have, by rejecting Soviet-style politics, accepted capitalist market ideologies and are now learning to cope with the free market. Thus, they accept proposals that fit within such an ideological framework, and are interested spectators in the battle between Europe and America to fine-tune these options. An interesting example is the debate on the supplementarity criteria. Under the different articles of the Protocol, the flexible mechanisms must be supplemental to domestic action. The developing countries and the green NGOs want the bulk of action, in principle, to be taken within the domestic context of the developed countries. The EU, taking a moral stand, also decided to favour the decision that at least 50 per cent of the emission reductions to be achieved by a country should be undertaken within that country. This, however, is not a cheap decision for the EU, and member countries are not evenly enthusiastic about it. The rest of the developed countries oppose it, arguing that if one accepts the cost-effectiveness principle then one should not make arbitrary limitations on the emission reduction to be achieved. Industry and business agree with the latter perspective. This was one of the points that led to the breakdown of the Hague talks in November 2000.

Another critical issue that affects preparations for international negotiations is the scientific preparation and analysis of key issues.

While some countries, such as the UK, US, Canada, Netherlands, Norway and Japan, have small battalions of scientific researchers analysing the issues from a range of perspectives and making policy-relevant recommendations, which are at least communicated to the policy-makers even if they are not always taken into account, this is hardly the case in the developing countries. Structural imbalance in the negotiations is the result of disparities in research, in terms of how much is sponsored and by whom; in terms of assumptions used and theories applied, which reflect vastly different scientific choices, ideological starting points and cultural differences; and in terms of extrapolation and interpretation of existing information (Gupta 1997; Kandlikar and Sagar 1999; Boehmer-Christiansen and Skea 1994; Agarwal and Narain 1991, 1992; Rao 1992). Scientific information generally goes through a process of peer review and improvement; Northern science, however, is rarely reviewed by Southern research-ers, and the normal process of checks and balances is missing. South-ern experts occasionally find mistakes or differ in their interpretation of certain research results. They then suspect all Northern literature of being biased against their interests. The IPCC 1996 working group 1, for instance, shows an imbalance as between US scientists (158), Indian (3) and Chinese (5) (Sagar and Kandlikar 1997).

Scientists and researchers in general have access to only part of the information. That access is limited by their world views and methodological constraints. When the information is put together, a larger picture seems to emerge. But different versions of the larger picture emerge for different scientists. That large picture can be interpreted in different ways, and different actors can use the infor-mation to suit their purposes.

The first key issue is that of scientific objectivity. Science does not really aim at objectivity, but at ensuring consistent results using a specific methodology, based on certain assumptions. It aims at ensur-ing that the results are reproducible by others under the same circum-stances. The scientific process is accompanied by a system of checks and balances. Publication in journals is possible only when peer reviewers find the articles sound, based on the given assumptions and methodologies used. At the same time, from a North–South

Box 19   Science and non-science

The development of scientific answers is so context-related that some-times one may be tempted to question not so much the integrity of the research but the relevance of the results to international decision-making. Some questions that arise in the context of the climate change discussions are:

- What are safe concentration levels of greenhouse gases and by when must such a level be reached? Why does the IPCC not explicitly come up with an answer on this issue instead of presenting it in terms of scenarios? Why is this a political question and not a sci-entific question? If every human being has human rights and if every country has the right to exist, then do not safe concentration levels mean that no human being or country's survival should be at risk? Why are lawyers focusing more on human rights violations as a result of political action and not on human rights violations as a result of political inaction?

- Why is it more legitimate to talk about the social costs of climate change than about the political costs (see Pearce *et al.* 1995; IPCC 1995)? Why can we talk about the costs of life, property and environ-ment, and not talk about the costs of losing countries, communi-ties and ecosystems? Why should death be measured in money and not in numbers?

- Why are fuels sold to aircraft and ships not calculated and ascribed to the countries that profit from these systems? Why are they seen as so complicated that they are not included in the calculations of emissions from individual countries? Why is this not a scientific question? Can the different social and natural sciences not come up with alternative systems for ascribing responsibilities and then com-paring these systems and making recommendations?

- Why are emissions from survival activities of the marginalised com-pared to emissions from luxury items (cf. Agarwal and Narain 1991)? Why is this not a scientific question? Is science incapable of distin-guishing between the two?

- Science depends on theories, methods and data. The choice of theoretical framework, methodology and data can influence the outcome of scientific research. How does one calculate the meth-ane emissions of a cow? One picks a standard animal and its emis-sions are then multiplied by the number of cows. But not all cows are the same; nor do they eat the same food. So how does one pick the standard animal (cf. Mitra 1992a)? Wet rice cultivation yields methane emissions. But the emissions depend on the type of soil and the quantity of the water available in the fields. So how does one assess the rice-related emissions in a number of countries with different circumstances (cf. Agarwal and Narain 1992)? How does one calculate the emissions from deforestation? Do all trees give out the same amount of emissions? What happens if the wood from the trees is used for furniture?

- Why does science find it so difficult to talk about equity? While philosophers and jurists have never hesitated in the past to discuss justice and equity, equity has increasingly become a highly loaded concept. With every discipline jumping in to discuss what equity is, the notion has become increasingly muddied and all kinds of definitions are being attributed to it from an objective scientific point of view. The open-mindedness with which equity is being dealt with can be contrasted with the rigidity with which cost-effectiveness is covered in the literature.

For more details see Gupta 1997: 150–68.

perspective, this often means that there is not enough scientific peer review from Southern scientists on Northern science.

The second key issue is scientific consensus. For some scientists, scientific integrity depends on the quality of the results and not on how many people agree with them. For others, scientific integrity is enhanced by discussing conflicting results from conflicting models and conflicting disciplines to see if an overall picture can emerge. They focus on the need for consensus between different strains of scientific thought. The IPCC is an example of the latter type of scientific thinking. Proponents of the former thought process find such consensus-seeking unscientific, more an activity for politicians.

The third key issue is scientific coverage. Science needs funding. Funders need reasons to justify expenditures. Inevitably this means that funding is channelled into those areas seen as likely to benefit national society as a whole, in terms of health or economy. But this often means that the social sciences get relatively few resources. This implies a strong focus on fundamental natural science, economics and technology, and less on the softer sciences, leading to skewed results when these are aggregated together. In the climate change negotiations this often means less focus on normative science – the

BOX 20 Legality and legitimacy

In general it is very difficult to ascertain the gap between the negotiating position and the positions of policy-makers and stakeholders in the domestic context, especially because of the reluctance of many developing country negotiators to commit themselves in writing. However, there is one anecdote that may be worth telling. This is the story of the opposition of some African countries to Joint Implementation. In the early days of the negotiations, the negotiators from these countries were making statements about their national position on the issue. In follow-up research to understand the precise nature of the opposition and conditions for support, researchers in the countries concerned were asked to meet with stakeholders, including policy-makers, to ascertain what they actually wanted.

At a follow-up research meeting in Harare, I presented the positions of the different countries as reflected in speeches made by their negotiators at the negotiations. The country researchers disagreed, saying that their countries had no positions in relation to the issue – and everything was in a state of flux. We all looked at the negotiators from the countries concerned, who were in the room. They kept their peace, neither denying that they had spoken out at the international negotiations, nor accepting that there was in fact no domestic position. Later discussions revealed that the negotiators faced a major dilemma. Given that issues in the international context proceed with rapidity, given that there is a cleavage between the importance given to issues at the international negotiations and complete indifference in the domestic context, the negotiators are left with a choice: accept a proposal by default (keeping quiet), or try to use their instincts to prepare a negotiating position that may be in line with national feeling on the subject. Keeping quiet is the easiest option, but commits their country to the negotiated agreement. Speaking up runs the risk of exposure back home and problems with superiors, and may even lead to risking job prospects. The choice of asking for more time to consider the issue on the negotiating table is not a real choice, since that would postpone negotiations indefinitely. Thus the negotiators had a perfectly legal position, but the legitimacy of their position was called into question (Gupta *et al.* 1996).

This anecdote shows that negotiators from individual countries are trying to use the negotiating process effectively, even though they do not necessarily have a specific mandate from their governments to do so. However, if a deal is finally made, there is no guarantee that the governments and stakeholders back home will accept it. This might lead to a huge waste of resources and undermine the credibility of the process. In theory, negotiators should come well prepared to the negotiations, having thought out a variety of responses. In practice, it is difficult to predict the dynamics, given the large number of countries and social actors participating; it is difficult to predict the issues that will be discussed in plenary and whether there will be sufficient time for negotiations. At the same time, the issues are so complex that preparing a well thought-out response on all the possible eventualities at the domestic level also appears impossible, given the low priority accorded to climate change in many developing countries.

need to work towards global stability and peace through economic and political reformation – and there is less science focusing on the interests and the challenges of the South. This also means that questions are sometimes defined more as political issues than scientific, and are therefore taken out of the purview of scientific analysis.

Ignorance of the facts hampers the assessment of national interests. As negotiations proceed, and discussions move rapidly and negotiating positions change, individual countries need to be ready with a range of reactions to alternative formulations of an existing package.

The example of emission trading is enlightening. The developing countries and the EU wanted targets for the developed countries at Kyoto. Emission trading was an option but the substantive discussions were lost in the debate on how emission rights should be allocated. When, at the last minute, targets were negotiated in conjunction with emission trading, it became very difficult for the developing countries to know how to respond. Were the targets worth the cost of the precedent of grandfathered emission allowances (see pp. 69–72)?

Another critical element missing in the process is domestic support for negotiating positions. While in general one can argue that domestic discussions should precede, and explicitly or implicitly support, a country's negotiating stance, this is not the case for much of the world. It is increasingly apparent that most people are blissfully unaware of the negotiating positions of their governments and are only afterwards informed, if at all, about the outcome (see Box 20).

However, while it is the developing countries in particular that face such dilemmas, it is not as if people in the developed countries

BOX 21   Legitimacy in the developed countries

The Netherlands: Credit and Credibility   A closer examination of the situation in the Netherlands is revealing. The self-image of the Dutch negotiator is that he or she fights for equity and environmental protection. This image has led the Dutch to take on a leadership role since the 1990s, arguing in favour of strong emission reductions and proposing a range of concepts and ideas to influence the international negotiating process. Meanwhile, the Dutch, who spearheaded the campaign towards the stabilisation target in the Climate Convention, have themselves failed to reach that goal and are today some 11–13 per cent above their 1990 emission levels. While once again arguing in favour of a −15 per cent target for Europe and a −10 per cent target for themselves in 1997, they finally accepted a −8 per cent for Europe and a −6 per cent target for themselves. There are also reports that although in principle the country supports the supplementarity principle, it secretly favours its rejection. Finally, to make matters worse, despite ostensibly strong leadership aspirations, the political coalition that came to power in 1998 announced that it would not ratify the Kyoto Protocol if the US and Japan did not. The conditional ratification builds negotiating space for the Dutch. If indeed the Dutch presidency of the negotiations has now succeeded in brokering a global compromise (minus the US) on the climate change issue, then it will be interesting to watch the internal dynamics of ratification.

The US: Pride and Prejudice   One may also argue that the changing position of the US government is highly revealing. After convincing the whole world to accept a range of flexibility mechanisms and agreeing only to targets, the then US President found himself facing a Republican majority likely to refuse to ratify the Kyoto Protocol even so. In the battle to win the 2000 presidential election, Bush announced that he would take measures to reduce greenhouse gas emissions. But when Bush came to power, he promptly announced his refusal to support the Protocol until the developing countries commit themselves actively to the process. However, since June 2001 he has himself faced a hostile majority in the Senate, and he may have to shift position again. By playing a relatively passive role in the negotiations at Bonn in July 2001, the US had further isolated itself, especially now that the rest of the world appears not only to have reached a compromise, but to be jubilant about having been able to do so. Will the Democratic majority in the Senate be pleased with the outcome?

do not. Sitting at home, trying to make sense of the decision taken on sinks on what may go down in history as that crucial day in Bonn that led to breakthrough and agreement, 23 July 2001, I found that it was extremely challenging to try and translate the decision into simple English. Apparently, the story going around was that even the Russian translator could not make sense of the complex jargon of the draft decision. Obviously it is difficult to respond to the heated pressure of negotiations if one does not know what people are talking about! The confusion one sees in the developing countries and possibly in many former Eastern Bloc countries is a stark version of what is happening frequently in the developed countries as well (see Box 21).

The considerable difference between countries in the quality and depth of their preparations for international negotiations is also reflected in the influence they have in drafting texts and papers. While the developed countries frequently come with draft protocol texts and documents for distribution, developing countries rarely do so.

AT THE NEGOTIATIONS: WHEN THE GOING GETS TOUGH

At the negotiations themselves, some countries come with a delegation of up to 150 people, others are represented by one or two negotiators. While some countries have enough delegates to cover the various issues and to work in shifts, other delegations have to cope with one or two people, who have to keep alert through simultaneous meetings and side events (where countries, NGOs and scientists present perspectives, positions and research results). The sheer imbalance in the teams leads to an imbalance in the negotiating process.

Inevitably the agenda gets dominated by those countries able to influence the negotiating process in the multiple forums where preparations take place. As a developing country interviewee put it: 'Although we participate – the point is not the breadth of the participation but the depth of it'.

Although climate change negotiations do not proceed fast enough for environmentalists, they are fairly rapid, cover a vast range of complicated issues and occur several times a year. In between these meetings, countries are expected to prepare for the negotiations. At the international negotiating process, in general, there are two formal plenary sessions and, when the going gets rough, these are suspended and several small informal groups established to negotiate key issues. In the climate change negotiations, there are a variety of such groups called the Friends of the Chair – working groups on specific issues, joint working groups, contact groups which are more ad hoc and are called to discuss new differences between parties, joint contact groups, and informal groups, where people can merely discuss as opposed to negotiate. The bulk of the work at the negotiations takes place in these groups, and when ready, a proposal is discussed in plenary sessions.

There are obvious advantages in having such groups. Clearly it is impossible to negotiate with 180-plus parties simultaneously on a large number of issues. These groups develop compromise texts and work towards understanding the views of other countries. They are absolutely vital to the negotiating processes and help to save time. However, informal sessions are mostly undertaken in English, and draft texts are prepared and discussed mostly in English among fluent English-speaking diplomats and lawyers. Non-English speakers find it extremely difficult to understand the process, let alone to influence it with better wording. This tends to marginalize non-English speakers and reduce transparency. While EU member states hope and rely on other member states to represent their positions, people from the countries with economies in transition and the developing countries face major disadvantages. For many developing countries and some Eastern and Central European countries, attending the different contact groups becomes impossible.

The complex nature of the discussions calls for experts in energy, forestry, finance and technology, let alone drafting experts, climatologists and diplomats, so that only delegations large enough to include all these experts are really able to participate effectively in the negotiations. Others try hard to keep up with the pace of the discussions and this is enormously complex. Very often they just give up.

In general, there are standard UN procedures that are followed at negotiations. Sometimes, these procedures are modified to fit the specific negotiations taking place. These rules cover issues such as how often meetings can take place, and who has responsibility for taking action in relation to these meetings. They discuss the rules of conduct in the meetings and who should chair and manage the issues and how the agenda should be developed.

In the absence of any specific decision, it is believed that decisions have to be taken by consensus rather than by majority voting. Consensus tends to mean that no one really objects to the formulation. The consensus rule gives power to individual countries that do not mind holding up the process by objecting to a specific decision. In effect, it gives veto power. But individual countries are generally afraid to object alone, because of the implications for social and diplomatic relations. Ultimately, it is usually only the US or an OPEC country such as Saudi Arabia that tends to object alone. EU member states try to object as a group, and so do G77 member states.

In order to avoid being captive to individual objectors, there is a majority rule that can be adopted. However, this rule might automatically transfer power to the developing countries, who are in the majority in the climate change negotiation. This is acceptable neither to the developed countries, nor to OPEC countries, who are not always in agreement with the other developing countries. The discussions in relation to the majority rule remain controversial. What is unique about the Bonn 2001 meeting is that the US did not use its veto power to block the proceedings.

Agreements are often drawn up after the negotiations have closed. At Kyoto, many delegates were on their way home when they heard on CNN that an agreement had been adopted. The Hague meeting, too, went beyond the planned closure time.

CONCLUSION

International negotiations have rules of procedure to guarantee the fairness of the proceedings. And yet the fairness is elusive. The form, as opposed to the substance, of cooperation has become so routine that developing countries appear only to go through the motions of participating in international treaties; they appear to be socialised into the process. There is some social learning taking place, but there is little input. Thus even though cooperation appears to have become institutionalised, this institutionalisation may be only skin deep. This will lead to increased frustration in the South, because of its inability to cope with the wide range of issues being discussed at international meetings, and the perception of interviewees that 'we are being asked to pay someone else's bill, that it will affect us in the next 5–10 years and these commitments will hurt'. Second, southern countries are becoming frustrated because they have a poor track record in implementing international agreements, and they are afraid that the continuation of such a trend is a foregone conclusion (cf. Birnie and Boyle 1992: 546; Young and Moltke 1994; Jacobson and Weiss 1995). Third, there is growing frustration that the international legal system, while promising the rule of law in terms of procedural issues, does not provide substantive guidance. There is a fear that legal principles of justice and fairness are not being developed, and instead the international legal system provides an arena for realpolitik, which then gets institutionalised by the legal power of precedents. Interviewees were afraid that the international legal process merely ensured 'polite order' within which the 'rules of the jungle' operated: 'The process conforms by default to legal processes; the process is a political one; fairness has to be fought for; it is not a right in the international process.' 'The entire international process is trying to maintain the international status quo in environment, trade and disarmament; the effort is to maintain an international status quo in all regimes that affect us.... Without equity we have instability and that is not in our interests. We are not fighting for equity because it is morally right, but because we want stability. The environmental disasters affect the poor first and the NGOs are working hard to influence these issues.' 'We mistrust the North and we spend all our time analysing their agenda rather than preparing ours' (see Gupta 2000a for details of the interviews).

But developed countries will also become frustrated by the relatively slow and defensive strategies used by the South to counter innovative and creative suggestions, by the lack of organisation and increasing lack of interest in the negotiations in the South, by the continued Southern default in meeting international commitments, and by the discovery that skilful negotiations in an orderly international system may lead to outputs that favour their interests, but do not lead to problem solving. If the developing countries are unable to come well prepared to the negotiating table, if they continue to show a poor record in implementation, these will be arguments likely to be used by some Northern countries to show that the developing countries are taking a free ride on the environmental policies of the North, and that action in the North should become conditional on action in the South.

Another question arises: is it sensible for the developing countries to participate in these types of international negotiations when they are sitting in a 'train with a fixed itinerary'? The answer is mixed. Interviewees argue that 'participating in these conventions may be in the long-run not beneficial to the South, but will be beneficial to the North. The North takes advantage of the process to push its interests through'. But there are others who see that not participating may be worse than participating, especially given the trends towards globalisation. Meanwhile, developing countries are falling behind in the negotiation process. 'How many rounds of loops can you get behind? Developing countries have to get their act together. Are governments going to govern or are they going to keep responding?'

CHAPTER 9

SAVING FACE
IS SAVING FAITH

The Gods help those that help themselves.
Aesop

THREE STEPS FORWARD, TWO STEPS BACK

That we live in a politically simmering planet is more than evident. Whether the climate is also simmering is less evident to those who like linear and straightforward causal reasoning and cannot cope with non-linearity, uncertainty, complex feed-back events and fear.

Do all the individual events taking place worldwide fit into a pattern? Even if that pattern matches the results of climate science's Global Circulation Models, does that mean we have a climate change problem? The consensus is that there is a problem. But some scientists argue that consensus in science is nonsense. The uncertainty provides the breeding ground for dissension over the issue, and the devil may cite the scripture to suit his purpose.

Nevertheless, 186 countries have joined forces to deal with this problem. They adopted the United Nations Framework Convention on Climate Change in 1992 and the Kyoto Protocol in 1997. This was based on the leadership paradigm: the rich were going to lead the way by reducing their own emissions *and* helping the South. Somewhere along the five-year journey, the rich got cold feet and began to find ways to reduce their own emissions by helping other countries through the flexibility mechanisms, which allow the developed to reduce emissions wherever it is most cost-effective to do so.

In 1998 it became increasingly clear that the United States of America would not ratify the Kyoto Protocol until the developing countries took action. The developing countries would not accept quantitative commitments until the developed countries themselves took action to limit the growth of their emissions. The European Union countries were not willing to ratify the Protocol till the United States and Japan did so. The leadership paradigm degraded to a conditional leadership paradigm.

In 2001, George W. Bush decided to put an end to the stalemate. The richest and most powerful nation in the world decided to play solitaire and withdraw support for the Kyoto Protocol. Bush announced that he was not going to ratify the agreement and instead launched a domestic energy programme that pleased the fossil fuel lobby and displeased environmentalists and the green business community. With his announcement, he created a flurry of activity in the rest of the developed world, with a number of countries secretly pleased at being relieved of their responsibilities, under the argument that if the US does not agree, then it makes no sense for us to agree.

However, political agreement between the rest of the world was achieved at the last meeting of the Conference of the Parties to the Climate Change Convention in July 2001, even though at a heavy price. Amidst a standing ovation at the compromise reached, there was a feeling of enormous relief that the rest of the world could dare to go ahead without the US. How long this collective defiance of the only global superpower will last is a matter of speculation. Ratification of the Kyoto Protocol is now expected to follow. Whether this is the beginning of the end of US hegemony in global politics and economics is a key question.

BONN 2001: PYRRHIC VICTORY

The Climate Convention of 1992 was merely a framework setting out in general terms what needs to be done. The Kyoto Protocol had much more in terms of legally binding quantitative commitments for the developed countries, but these were dissipated through the adoption of flexible mechanisms and options. Thus, the targets were unambitious to begin with, focused on additional gases; sinks were included, and countries were allowed to participate in Emission Trading, Joint Implementation and the Clean Development Mechanism. The combined effect of all these options weakened the effect of the commitments and the incentive that it provided for the development of new technologies. The developing country demands for technology transfer and financial assistance appeared to fall on deaf ears.

The simmering disagreements rose to the surface at the Hague meeting, which broke down over the issues of sinks, flexibility mechanisms, financial support to developing countries and compliance mechanisms. Surprisingly, with the US withdrawal from the Protocol negotiations, political agreement was reached at Bonn on all these issues. Funds were established, rules on flexibility mechanisms, sinks and compliance negotiated. Of course more work needs to be done before these become legally binding. But still there was a feeling of jubilation.

And yet, what does this all mean? Contribution to the funds is mainly voluntary. Will countries be forthcoming with resources for yet more funds when they have been relatively reluctant donors in the past? The use of sinks, still poorly understood, will reduce the pressure to take action where it really counts – that is, to push countries towards low greenhouse gas technologies. The rules on the flexibility mechanisms did not really meet developing country concerns. Clearly any agreement is better than no agreement. But what if the non-participation of the US implies that the world's largest polluter and highest per capita polluter can simply get away with it because of its power and lack of responsibility? The US becomes then the 'rogue state' in global climate policy. And all the concessions made to bring all countries on board may have weakened the treaty even further. Is this a pyrrhic victory?

In the long process of negotiation, the next step is always to build cautiously on earlier steps. Ratification needs to follow rapidly and the lines of communication in the rest of the world need to be kept open. If the Protocol enters into force in 2001, there will be enough messages for at least non-US industry to take action, and they will have enough flexibility either to take the opportunities that come their way or to seize the loopholes if the opportunities fail. NGOs and civil society will probably have to keep the pressure up. Experimentation with the sinks and flexibility mechanisms will lead to further fine-tuning of the definitions in the coming negotiations on the second commitment period.

THE PROBLEM REDEFINED: IDEOLOGICAL, TECHNOLOGICAL AND INSTITUTIONAL 'LOCK-IN'

Is climate change a problem of emissions or is it a problem about our production and consumption patterns? In many ways it is both. It can be defined narrowly as a problem about emissions, but when the emissions need to be reduced as drastically as suggested by the key scientific reports, inevitably this means that it is a problem about our production and consumption patterns and our very lifestyles.

However, discussion of lifestyles and ideologies tends to be extremely sensitive. President Bush senior clearly stated at UNCED in 1992 that as far as he was concerned the American way of life cannot be compromised. His son seems to take an extreme view on this issue. There is hope that somehow liberalism and the free market will pave the way to environmental emancipation. While in Europe there is increasing recognition that market forces must operate within a basic environmental framework, in many other countries this realisation is being downplayed. The timing is also unfortunate. The liberalised world has just begun to celebrate its victory over communism, only to discover that the seeds of decay may also be evident in capitalism and globalisation. Infused with success and armed with formulae, the Bretton Woods institutions have gone to the developing countries to convince them that neoliberalism is the way forward and the markets should open up, subsidies should be phased out, and countries should embrace the new ideology. But, as argued in Chapter 1, globalisation may be the new colonialism and the good intentions behind globalisation may not work out quite as its wellwishers hope.

Although there are many who see the need for environmental protection, we seem to be locked into an economic and political ideology which focuses on short-term economic gain. At UNCED, countries could not find a way out of this dilemma (Chatterjee and Finger 1994: 172). 'The necessity for new models of wealth, sustainable and copyable ways of life is diametrically opposed to present reality, and yet it is inescapable' (Weiszäcker *et al.* 1998: 205). The problem too is that with industrialisation, the structure of industry and society get interlocked. As the industrial systems progress there are successions of interlocking technologies and each new system builds on the earlier system (Womack *et al.* 1990; Grubler 1994; Mokyr 1994). This locking-in process resists change, even though there may be recognition of the need for change.

Developed countries and the sirens: the myth of staying in control

While the developed countries would like to think of themselves as very much in control, as the ones with the answers to global problems and the formulae for global development, they are clearly afraid to look in the mirror. If they did, they would see themselves as prisoners of political short-term time-frames, share markets, ideological and technological lock-in: so locked into their current way of life and so egoistic that they dare not admit defeat by a larger and more complex problem. There is inadequate self-reflection on the consequences of the system being set up. Countries and societies are becoming locked into the development mode, and lives, processes and systems are linked with everything else. Change is seen as problematic because it affects the competitiveness of industry, which in turn affects national income and well-being. Countries are becoming extremely vulnerable in that they are dependent on a whole chain of reactions when action is taken; thus everyone settles for incremental change and the status quo. They are so rich, they discount the future and gamble on being the winner. The former Eastern Bloc countries cannot wait to see themselves take on the same image. With the decay of communism, the glamour of the free market beckons, and, stumbling on their way, they too pursue the path of capitalism in the hope that it will lead to wealth and glory. The developed countries are not taking time to think that in an ever-shrinking world, the problems of the developing countries may boomerang on them.

The music of the sirens lures them on.

Developing countries: wallowing in self-pity

At the same time, the developing countries are articulating old grudges and wallowing in self-pity and pathetic excuses for not taking action. As long as they show themselves to be weak and disunited they will be raped and plundered at worst, and considered irrelevant and pathetic at best. It is time for them to stand up for themselves and to fight for what they want.

The developing countries face the dilemmas of modernising without westernising; surviving economically without squandering natural resources; requesting financial and technological help without mortgaging the future; allowing the giant transnational corporations in without sacrificing public priorities; demanding fairness and equity from the North without guaranteeing it domestically; and fighting for short-term economic gain without incurring long-term loss.

Let us now return to diversity in the South. Although there is considerable uncertainty about the statistics, there are some very rich 'developing' countries, such as Singapore and Qatar. These are as rich as the richest countries in the world and yet they are part of the G77, and support their position of not making quantitative legally binding commitments under the climate treaties. Are some developing countries misusing their membership of the G77 at the cost of G77's credibility?

North–South relations: frustration breeds frustration

In the increasingly tense relations between the North and the South, there is also a sense of frustration. On the part of the South this reflects an inability to prepare and negotiate effectively, to fight the tendencies that maintain the status quo, and to prevent new precedents being set that work against their long-term interests. It reflects fear that no real solutions for a range of social and environmental problems, which have been on the international agenda for a long time, have been developed. The South also feels that it is being manoeuvred into accepting compromises that it does not want to accept and that the normative function of law is being marginalised.

None of this makes it easier on the North. It too is getting fed up with the threadbare, defensive and rhetorical strategies of the South and its inability to suggest workable solutions. This leads some experts to argue that using a North–South framework inevitably leads to failure in treaty-making, because the South brings up all its grudges. 'And within that framework, the nexus between indebtedness, poverty and the conditionality of transfers is an unproductive starting point for the discussion of policy options' (Pearce and Perrings 1995: 24). Others argue that the North–South framework is the only real framework for discussions, because most environmental problems are inescapably linked with problems of inequality.

THE SCENARIOS

The ostrich phenomenon

But is there really a climate change problem? Or, given the enormous difficulties in addressing the problem, do we conclude that there is no problem and bury our heads in the sand?

Chapter 2 argued that there is increasing evidence of a climate change problem. But there is also uncertainty. Most of us like to live our lives in an orderly fashion and proceed from the notion of certainty. But modern life is increasingly about uncertainty. We know that cigarette smoking can cause cancer, but does living near a nuclear reactor cause cancer and birth defects? Can the causal elements be separated to determine a linear relationship between cause and effect? And if there is uncertainty does that mean that we should not take any action? This policy dilemma has been discussed over and over again, and has ultimately led to the adoption of the so-called precautionary principle.

In 1987, the World Commission on Environment and Development stated in its report, *Our Common Future*, 'How much certainty should governments require before agreeing to take action? If they wait until significant climate change is demonstrated, it may be too late for any counter-measures to be effective against the inertia by then stored in this massive global system' (Brundtland *et al.* 1987).

This concept was used in the Declaration of the Second World Climate Conference, which stated: 'In order to achieve sustainable development in all countries and to meet the needs of present and future generations, precautionary measures to meet the climate challenge must anticipate, prevent, attack, or minimise the causes of, and mitigate the adverse consequences of, environmental degradation that might result from climate change'.

The precautionary principle is defined in the United Nations Framework Convention on Climate Change as

> measures to anticipate, prevent or minimize the causes of climate change and mitigate its adverse effects. Where there are threats of serious or irreversible damage, lack of full scientific certainty should not be used as a reason for postponing such measures, taking into account that policies and measures to deal with climate change should be cost-effective so as to ensure global benefits at the lowest possible cost. To achieve this, such policies and measures should take into account different socio-economic contexts, be comprehensive, cover all relevant sources, sinks and reservoirs of greenhouse gases and adaptation, and comprise all economic sectors. Efforts to address climate change may be carried out cooperatively by interested Parties.

This principle provides policy-makers and politicians with the ammunition to take action when there is evidence of an irreversible effect, even if the effect is uncertain. From an environmental perspective this argument makes perfect sense. From a legal perspective, it is a vital first step and yet it is so open to interpretation that it does not say very much (cf. Freestone and Hey 1996). However, other policy-makers may argue that the precautionary principle justifies action only when the costs of dealing with the potential irreversible impacts are less than the costs of taking measures now. From an economic perspective this argument makes perfect sense. It seems ludicrous to spend large sums of money to avert a possible crisis, the impacts of which are relatively negligible economically for that society.

This inevitably brings us into the realm of speculation about the likely costs and who is likely to have to bear them. The huge controversy that surrounded the chapter in the Second Assessment

Report of the IPCC on the costs to human life of the potential impacts of climate change has led to a situation where scientists are increasingly shying away from making global cost estimates. Apart from the scientific dilemma of how to ascertain the costs of possible policies now, there are always greater difficulties in ascertaining likely future costs.

But more than that, the issue is who has to bear the costs, now and in the future. This gives a decided North–South twist to the discussions. If IPCC is correct in its assessment, and if there is a moderate increase in global temperatures, then it is likely that the bulk of the problems will be experienced in the South. Why then should the North take policy measures likely to affect its energy systems, production processes and transport systems, and hence national incomes and its ability to compete globally, when the likely economic impact in the long term is relatively low? There may of course be some impact in terms of the North's ability to sell produce in developing countries, but how significant is that? And there may be large numbers of environmental refugees, but under current policies only political refugees are allowed into the developed world, and environmental refugees are not political refugees, are they? On the other hand, if there is more than a moderate increase in global warming, the developed countries too will suffer. But how likely is that eventuality? For the South, this unfortunately implies that although not the major contributor to the problem, it is likely to be the major victim and does not have the wherewithal to deal with it.

Industrial transformation for the developed world

There are a number of positive ways out of the dilemma that climate change poses. The key solution is to decouple the emissions of green-house gases from the factors that lead to economic growth. This calls for new systems of production and consumption, a global phase-out of fossil fuels, and fuel substitution through sustainable renewable forms of energy. This is referred to in the economic literature as the environmental Kuznets curve. This curve implies that as countries become richer and more developed, the societies undergo structural change and their increasing wealth makes it possible to invest in more environmentally friendly technologies and lifestyles. This curve has been demonstrated by empirical evidence for a number of individual, local and regional pollutants. In such situations, the local population faces immediate benefits from policies to deal with the pollutants.

But although in theory the world could move to a GHG-free state, in practice public support for such risky political measures may be forthcoming only in the aftermath of a climate-related tragedy in the vicinity. The key challenge thus far is that although efficiency sounds attractive, it appears that there is a limit to the extent to which a society can become efficient. Mere growth in wealth leads to increases in demand, and that in itself leads to increased energy use.

Nevertheless, this is the only attractive model. In translating this model for developed and developing countries, the concepts of Factor Four and Factor Ten have been devised. Factor Four calls for doubling productivity while halving energy and resource use. Factor Ten calls for intensifying the rate of productivity and decreasing the rate of energy and resource use to make space for the developing countries to grow (Weiszäcker 1998; cf. Sachs *et al.* 1998). Factor Ten is based on the argument that the developed countries have caused the problem, and that they have the resources and technologies to undertake the switch towards industrial transformation, with its modified production and consumption systems and changed lifestyles. Fussler and James (1996) argue that sustainable technologies exist and are being developed rapidly. However, companies are being careful about introducing these technologies for fear of being in advance of consumer demand. Industry is caught in inertia and it is difficult for it to escape unless it gets clear signals from government (Byé 1997).

There are other reasons for the developed world to take action. There are, after all, benefits in a world that is not racked by poverty, distress and civil disruption. However easy it may appear to be to close the door on environmental refugees, this will not be easily reconcilable with the conscience of civil society, especially if the global media report it. As and when renewable technologies become economically viable, other governments will see the attractiveness of gaining a foothold in the developing countries through marketing such technologies. The number of jobs may increase over the years. It is always useful to have a rich market to sell one's produce to. Finally, as Jung and Loske (2000) argue, there is a major peace dividend in moving towards renewable energy, as the oil producers in the world are mostly locked up in war games.

But all this calls for brave statesmanship on the part of the leaders of powerful countries. They have to recognise that green industry and civil society are interested in the issue and that the public may well be willing to support climate change measures. An opinion poll in Japan in June 1997 revealed that 86 per cent of those polled were concerned about climate change and 84 per cent felt that emission reductions should take place even if there is a cost to the economy. A WWF poll in the US showed that 72 per cent of those surveyed were willing to accept a protocol with substantial cuts (20 per cent) of greenhouse gases by 2005.

Opportunities for the developing world

At the same time, the key challenge is the fact that the developed countries are locked, both ideologically and technologically, into a way of life. There are very strong vested interests that fight transformation because of the potential impacts for themselves. Sociologists argue that precisely for this reason, it is actually developing countries that have the potential space for change. They are mostly in a state of transformation, and in such societies there is more room to manoeuvre. Less developed countries could provide the so-called 'greenfield' economies that allow space for the interlinked innovations in social and industrial organisation that a sustainable industrial paradigm would require. There are vested interests, but these societies are not as locked in as Western societies. These greenfield economies could adopt technologies and know-how as long as there was support from the public policy framework, and financial and human resources were available (Wallace 1996). Although many newly industrialising countries have grown more from capital investment than from technological innovation, organisational competence and routines (Kim and Lau 1994), there are some examples of such leapfrogging. Thus developing countries are using mobile phones in advance of laying telephone cables in the ground. But before such systems can be effectively implemented, it is necessary to have national systems of innovation in place to encourage the selection of appropriate technologies. In the final analysis, it is simply a choice. Each society will have to choose its own path towards transformation. But there is plenty of potential for winning coalitions between NGOs, developmental organisations, green industry and environmental ministries. If the pressure is turned up, all industry will have to respond.

At the same time, there are plenty of other reasons to justify action by both developed and developing countries. The use of energy generated from locally available renewable sources immediately implies a reduced dependence on raw materials from other parts of the country and from other countries. This reduces the operational costs of producing energy and reduces the drain on scarce foreign exchange reserves. It also has the potential of reducing the other negative environmental impacts of power and energy generation. Wind energy is becoming economically competitive in different parts of the world, and there is considerable potential here. Small hydro and solar energy are also interesting opportunities for the future. Energy conservation too has enormous potential. Recent research reveals that both China and India can reduce their energy demands by at least 30 per cent over the next 20 years, by adopting energy-efficient technologies and building codes (Gupta *et al.* 2001b). This can save money and resources for consumers and governments.

Many of the new industrial transformation challenges bring new jobs and opportunities for the entrepreneur. It is precisely in addressing such challenges that the developing countries could perhaps become forerunners in technology development. In fields where the North has long had competence, developing countries will have difficulties competing; it is in the new fields that they could develop the competitive edge. Young Indian and Chinese computer experts are already demonstrating their skills in this field, and are much in demand in the developed countries of the West.

Another reason for trying to leapfrog is that the copy-cat attitude – we will pollute because you polluted – serves no long-term goal. The developing countries already have so many problems to cope with that it does not make sense to multiply these by adding that of climate change to the list. Righteous indignation and wrath towards the first world does not help, because as long as the developing countries do not have the ability to negotiate effectively in a world ruled by power politics, they will be unable to convince the North of its liability. Besides, the righteous indignation tends to fade away as soon as the developing country itself reaches a level of economic maturity.

A key argument often made is that the links made by the South to debt, poverty abatement, trade and financial negotiations are too complex, and overburden the climate change negotiations; the South should not see the climate change problem as a mechanism to address all these other issues. This, I would argue, is a typically short-sighted approach to the problem. Although there is elegance in keeping the problem simple, the problem is not simple and is, unfortunately or fortunately as the case may be, intimately linked to a range of other issues. 'Climate policy will fail if it does not serve concrete interests and pursue several goals; it will also fail, in a different way, if it solves a problem that does not exist' (Boehmer Christiansen 1999: 395).

WINNER TAKES ALL: CYNICAL ISSUE LINKAGES

There will be winners and losers. But can the winners maximise their profits? There are some cynical issue linkages that may make it extremely profitable for the winner to optimise his profits:

- Nuclear energy – the rise of the phoenix. Some of the potential winners believe that they can profit from the situation by making an issue linkage with nuclear energy. Nuclear energy has low greenhouse gas emissions (except in the mining of uranium). This has provided a new boost to the nuclear industry and to governments that have long supported nuclear research. The potential for exporting nuclear technology from Canada, France and the USA would somehow lighten the burden that climate change may bring with it. This is indeed a cynical linkage and is based on the convenient assumption that developing countries like China, India and South Africa may well be willing to tread this path at the cost of having nuclear waste to dispose of. At the same time, this option appears to be partially ruled out by the recent decision at COP–6, part II, that credits from nuclear facilities are not to go to investor countries.

- The 'polluter gets paid' principle. In law people who cause harm to others are in general liable. In the international pollution discussions, this responsibility is translated into the polluter pays principle. However, in recent global negotiations, there is a tendency to assume that everyone is equally liable and hence instead of liability, countries and people should take action to the extent that they can afford and are willing to do so. In the climate change negotiation, instead of the United States having to pay the highest amount as the largest polluter at both gross and per capita levels, it has acquired a large assigned amount under the Kyoto Protocol which it can, if it wishes, trade in return for money. The polluter pays principle has metamorphosed into the polluter gets paid principle.

- Climate currency. There is now a new market and a new currency. There is room for technology developers to access new resources and to increase their wealth. Companies are already advertising the sales of CO_2 rights. NIBO, a Dutch international forestry organisation recently published an advertisement stating: 'NIBO NV offers the CO_2 rights based on newly established trees in exchange for financial inputs. Moreover, financers will receive a percentage of the future incomes of the plantations. Through this mechanism, the purchase of CO_2 offsets becomes a financially rewarding investment as well. The plantations will be established according to FSC [Forest Stewardship Council] principles and criteria. Maintenance and the annually sequestered amount of CO_2 will be verified by an independent third party' (JIQ 2001: 3). At the sixth Conference of the Parties in the Hague, environmental NGOs were circulating a new currency note. In dollar green, one side proclaimed: 'The history of colonialism goes in parallel with the creation of new commodities... slavery... sugar... tea... coffee ... oil... carbon?' The other side reads: '1 carbon credit... the value of the credit will go up and down according to global market speculation and is at no time and under any circumstances in any way related to any known concept or estimate of the ecological cost of industrial and corporate behaviour.... May be exchanged for nuclear power station, genetically modified forest or other similarly destructive project. This bill is solely for the purpose of increasing corporate profit and should not be considered as a viable solution to climate change.' There is thus money to be made for the climate brokers!

- Technology control. Since the bulk of the technologies that can address the climate change problem are primarily in the hands of the developed countries, the climate change issue provides these developers with a captive market worldwide. Who defines the technologies that are suitable? Those who have nuclear technology want to market it; those who have gas technologies want to market them. Who is to decide objectively what is most appropriate for the global community? The northern countries' technological lock-in is now being marketed to the South.

SAVING FACE

The problem is thus that we are all locked into a mindset, and thinking and acting differently poses challenges we do not dare to face. And yet this will be the major test in the coming years.

Re-thinking the South: coming to grips with reality

Clearly the developing countries have not had it easy. Their history of colonialism, slavery, poverty and disempowerment has made them see themselves as victims who can do nothing but face up to realpolitik by taking what they can get. But the role of victim serves no end. Developing countries need to take the following issues into account:

- Assess the opportunities outside the negotiations. There are opportunities for greenfield societies to adopt modern technologies and leapfrog into the twenty-first century. If mobile telephones can replace the telephone lines that were never laid, if modern computers can replace the old ones that had not been bought, then why cannot decentralised renewable energy systems replace the centralised fossil-fuel power plants and systems that are yet to be built? Developing countries may also find that they can themselves develop technologies that can compete globally. Research in China and India shows that these two countries at least have sufficient numbers of domestic reasons to invest in energy efficiency, energy conservation and renewable energy. The fact that they can as a result also contribute to the global climate change issue is a bonus.

- Reconsider who qualifies as a developing country. As Chapter 6 shows, the current divisions between rich and poor are so blurred by existing memberships in both groups that the legitimacy and credibility of the developing country position is at stake in the international negotiations.

- List, evaluate and assess the strengths of developing countries in the negotiations. The developing countries frequently adopt defensive and rhetorical positions consistent with the view that they are victimised in global politics. This ends up leading to self-fulfilling prophecies. Instead, they need to list their strengths and assess their strategies accordingly. This means, for example, that they should point out that the negative side-effects of climate change can boomerang back on the North by reducing the purchasing power of the South, increasing the civil crises in developing countries and thus the numbers of ecological refugees. They should also realise that they have considerable demographic and resource power that must be reckoned with.

- Develop coalitions with like-minded countries. Instead of coalescing with regional partners on the basis of historical relations, the developing countries should actively explore the possibilities of identifying partner countries on the basis of common interests in specific negotiations.

- Assess the opportunities in negotiations. There are opportunities within the treaty negotiations such as the controversial Clean

Development Mechanism and the Global Environment Facility, which can be used to their advantage, but only if there is a strategic policy focused on doing so.

RE-THINKING THE NORTH: THE CRACKED MIRROR

For the rich and powerful Northern countries, it is difficult to acknowledge that they are caught in an ideological, financial, technological and institutional lock-in. Accustomed to seeing themselves as free defenders of democracy and civil rights, they find it difficult to see that they and their economies are locked into systems and lifestyles that cannot easily be changed; that they are not, in fact, in control of their economies and lives, nor can they respond effectively and immediately to new challenges. Eastern and Central Europeans appear to be so blinded by the wealth and prosperity of the West that they have not yet realised that all that glistens is not gold. Although for Europeans there is a consciousness of the complex love–hate relationship with former colonies, Americans tend to be oblivious to the complexities of North–South relations, and the new US president, blithely unconscious of the social and global learning experiences of the last thirty years, is all set to rewrite history by changing US policy in relation to the ballistic missile treaty, the biological weapons treaty and the climate change treaty. While arguing that the precautionary principle does not justify high costs for the US in the climate change issue, he implicitly uses the same principle to justify the defence shield against so-called rogue states! But there will be a heavy price to pay for Bush's isolationist strategy: for Europe if it does not shake itself out of its inferiority complex and try to deal with the problems as it sees fit, and for Eastern and Central Europe if it does not try to think for itself. For the North, it is thus necessary:

- to take some time for introspection and to understand the driving forces of wealth and welfare within their own economies;
- to consider the potential for adopting Factor Ten policies and to demonstrate statesmanship in developing policies that can change the world. This calls for the adoption of strategies that promote industrial transformation;

- to realise that globalisation implies a bird's eye view of the whole world, and calamities that occur at the other end of the globe have a strange way of coming home to roost.

Rethinking North–South relations

Dealing as we are with nearly two hundred countries, it is inevitable that the world will be divided into groups, and rich and poor are as good a classification as any other, besides having stood the test of time. However, for such relations to improve, it is necessary that there is:

- Structured dialogue between both parties to induce social learning, mutual respect, understanding and forgiveness based on a system similar to the 'truth and reconciliation' approach, in order to build the necessary social capital and mutual trust. This will lead to better coalition building, better development of institutions and lowered transaction costs.

- Effective and principled negotiations where principles are the basis for determining responsibility and action and where there is enhanced transparency. This would, for example, imply the adoption of the 'polluter pays' principle: subject to the ability to pay the poorest countries would be exempted from action but assisted to adapt to the potential consequences of climate change; other developing countries would be *encouraged* to take action in a particular direction, but not *cornered*. This would also imply that those countries that 'graduate' into a particular classification and thus become eligible to take on certain measures are given a grace period or time-lag to allow them to respond. Countries that try and take measures outside their own national boundaries should be subject to a flexibility tax and countries that fail to comply with their commitments should have to pay a fine, which could then be used to generate resources for adaptation.

- Acceleration strategies that build on the issue-links of the weak. The weakest links in the chain are the developing countries, and in order to motivate them it is important to take their issue-linkages into account and build solutions around them. This might mean giving due importance to the issues of debt cancellation, trade barriers and tariffs, closing tax havens, and so on.

- Strategies to ensure that the developing countries have a fair chance in the negotiating process. This calls for legal aid for the poorest nations; deepening their degree of participation in negotiations; having shorter, fewer and more concise meetings within a rigid time-table, so that countries are not tired out by the negotiations; and the right of access to counter-science whenever the country is faced with foreign scientific evidence about its own role.

EPILOGUE

Is there then a problem of climate change, or do we recognize it only when we can afford such a problem because the solutions are suddenly attractive? Or does the global community still think that the solution lies in life-boat politics: rich countries save themselves, and the rest save themselves if they can. The concept of the 'tragedy of the commons' began as a simple discussion of overusing grazing rights in the local commons. Today, we are witnessing the tragedy of the global commons, unless we learn to cooperate in dealing with this problem.

One can generate a number of scenarios about the future of the global community. The ostrich approach focuses on decoupling global warming from greenhouse gas emissions or denying that the problem is serious enough to justify action. The Fort North approach decouples the right of growth from sovereignty. Thus not all countries have the right to growth. Given that there are limited resources and strong vested interests, Hardin's (1974) life-boat theory can be re-incarnated as Fort North. In such a situation the growth of the South is restricted by the international financial, economic, trade and political systems. This is the fear that developing countries are constantly grappling with. The industrial transformation approach focuses on decoupling emissions from economic growth through primarily technological growth and institutional support. The solidarity approach decouples emissions from the status quo; in this model, equity takes a central role and countries try to share the limited environmental utilisation space.

The life-boat theories are difficult to reconcile with the goals of the United Nations Charter; the equity theories are politically difficult and may be impossible to implement, especially in developed countries. The symbolic approach, which calls for a denial of the environmental problem, is not very responsible in the face of the growing evidence of pollution. The only attractive option of the four for all countries is the industrial transformation option, but this calls for a quantum leap of faith in modern technologies. As Clinton put it: 'If we do it right, protecting the climate will yield not costs, but profits; not burdens, but benefits; not sacrifice, but a higher standard of living' (Clinton 1997).

REFERENCES

Agarwal, A. (2000). *Making the Kyoto Protocol Work: Ecological and Economic Effectiveness and Equity in the Climate Regime*, CSE Statement, New Delhi.

Agarwal, A., J. Carabias, M.K.K. Peng, A. Mascarenhas, T. Mkandawire, A. Soto, E. Witoelar (1992). *For Earth's Sake: A Report from the Commission on Developing Countries and Global Change*, International Development Research Centre, Ottawa.

Agarwal, A. and S. Narain (1991). *Global Warming in an Unequal World: A Case of Environmental Colonialism*, Centre for Science and Environment, New Delhi.

Agarwal, A. and S. Narain (1992). *Towards a Green World: Should Global Environmental Management be Built on Legal Conventions or Human Rights*, Centre for Science and Environment, New Delhi.

Agenda 21 (1992). Report on the UN Conference on Environment and Development, Rio de Janeiro, 3–14 June 1992, UN doc. A/CONF.151/26/Rev.1 (Vols. I–III).

Agrawala, S. and S. Andresen (2001). Evolution of the Negotiating Positions of the United States in the Global Climate Change Regime, *Energy and Environment*.

Albright, M. (1998). Earth Day Speech to Combat Climate Change, held in the Museum of Natural History on April 21.

Alves, J. (1989). Statement of Brazil, in P. Vellinga, P. Kendall, and J. Gupta (eds.) *Noordwijk Conference Report*, Volume II, Ministry of Housing, Physical Planning and Environment, Netherlands, pp. 56–59.

Amin, S. (1993). The Challenge of Globalisation, in South Centre (ed.) *Facing the Challenge; Responses to the Report of the South Commission*, Zed Books, London, pp. 132–8.

Arnold, G. (1993). *The End of the Third World*, Macmillan, Basingstoke.

Asaoka, M. (1997). Toward COP–3: The View of an Environmental NGO, *Climate Change Bulletin*, 15.

Birnie, P.W. and A.E. Boyle (1992). *International Law and Environment*, Clarendon Press, Oxford.

Boehmer-Christiansen, S. (1999). Epilogue: Scientific Advice in the World of Power Politics, in P. Martens and Jan Rotmans (eds.) *Climate Change – An Integrated Perspective*, Kluwer Academic Publishers, Dordrecht, pp. 357–405.

Boehmer-Christiansen, S. and J. Skea (1994). *The Operation and Impact of the Intergovernmental Panel on Climate Change*, STEEP Paper 16, Programme on Environmental Policy and Regulation, Science Policy Research Unit, University of Sussex, Falmer.

Bolin, B. (1998). The Kyoto Negotiations on Climate Change: A Science Perspective, *Science*, pp. 330–31.

Brundtland, G.H. *et al.* (1987). *Our Common Future*, The World Commission on Environment and Development, Oxford University Press, Oxford.

Byé, P. (1997). Productive Inertia and Technical Change, in P. Byé, J.J. Chanaron and A. Richards (eds.) *Industrial History and Technological Development in Europe: Research Papers of the European Science and Technology Forum*, The Newcomen Society and the Science Museum, London.

CEO (2000). *Greenhouse Market Mania: UN Climate Talks Corrupted by Corporate Pseudo Solutions*, Corporate Europe Observatory, Amsterdam.

Chatterjee, P and M. Finger (1994). *The Earth Brokers*, Routledge, London.

Chengappa, R. (1992). The Tower of Babble, *India Today*, 30 June, pp. 30–32.

Claussen, E. (2000). Thoughtful Solutions Needed, *International Herald Tribune*, 18–19 November, p. 13.

Clinton, W.J. (1997). Remarks by the President on Global Climate Change, National Geographic Society, 22 October.

Dadzie, K.K.S. (1993). National and International Policies for Development, in South Centre (ed.) *Facing the Challenge: Responses to the Report of the South Commission*, Zed Books, London, pp. 230–36.

Dahl, A. (2000). Competence and Subsidiarity, in J. Gupta and M. Grubb (eds.) *Climate Change and European Leadership: A Sustainable Role for Europe*, Environment and Policy Series, Kluwer Academic Publishers, Dordrecht.

Dasgupta, C. (1994). The Climate Change Negotiations, in I.M. Mintzer and J.A. Leonard (eds.) *Negotiating Climate Change: The Inside Story of the Rio Convention*, Cambridge University Press, Cambridge, pp. 129–48.

David, G.V. and J.E. Salt (1995). Keeping the Climate Treaty Relevant, *Nature*, 373, p. 280.

De La Perrière, R.A.B. and F. Seurat (2000). *Brave New Seeds: The Threat of GM Crops to Farmers*, Zed Books, London.

De Rivero, O. (2001). *The Myth of Development*, Zed Books, London.

EAJ *et al.* (2000). Sinking the Kyoto Protocol: Position Paper on the Exclusion of Land Use, Land Use Change and Forestry (LULUCF) Projects in the Kyoto Mechanisms, Earthlife Africa Johannesburg, Environmental Monitoring Group, Group for Environmental Monitoring, Greater Edendale Environmental Network, South African Climate Action Network, Johannesburg.

Eizenstat, S. (1998). Eizenstat Addresses Climate Change Treaty Concerns, Speech of the Under Secretary of State on 14 April to the Association of Women in International Trade.

Freestone, D. and E. Hey (eds.) (1996). *Precautionary Principle: Book of Essays*, Environmental Policy and Law Series, Kluwer Law International, The Hague.

Fussler, C. and P. James (1996). *Driving Eco-Innovation: A Breakthrough Discipline for Innovation and Sustainability*, Pitman, London.

Fussler, C. (1998). Dow Europe: Six Sustainability Rules for a Complex World, in P. Vellinga, F. Berkhout and J. Gupta (eds.) *Managing a Material World: Reflections on Industrial Ecology*, Environment and Policy Series, Kluwer Academic Publishers, Dordrecht, pp. 267–74.

Galtung, J. (1993). People Centred Development through Collective Self Reliance, in South Centre (ed.) *Facing the Challenge: Responses to the Report of the South Commission*, Zed Books, London, pp. 132–8.

George, S. (1992). *The Debt Boomerang: How Third World Debt Harms Us All*, Pluto Press, London.

Globe International Press Release (1998). Buenos Aires Conference Finishes with Clear Steps to the Future, Press Release dated 14 November, Globe International Secretariat, Brussels.

Goldemberg, J. (1994). The Road to Rio, in I.M. Mintzer and J.A. Leonard (eds.) *Negotiating Climate Change: The Inside Story of the Rio Convention*, Cambridge University Press, Cambridge, pp. 175–87.

Gore, A. (1992). *Earth in the Balance: Ecology and the Human Spirit*, Plume Book.

Gosovic, B. (1992). *The Quest for World Environmental Cooperation: The Case of the UN Global Environment Monitoring System*, Routledge, London, pp. 223–71.

Greenpeace (1994). *The Climate Time Bomb: Signs of Climate Change from the Greenpeace Data Base*, Greenpeace International, Amsterdam.

Group of 77 South Summit (2000). Declaration of the South Summit, Havana, 10–14 April.

Grubb, M., C. Vrolijk and D. Brack (1999). *The Kyoto Protocol*, Earthscan/ RIIA, London.

Grubb, M. and F. Yamin (2001). Climatic Collapse at The Hague: What Happened, Why and Where Do We Go From Here?, *International Affairs*, Vol. 77, No. 2, pp. 261–76.

Grubler, A. (1994). Industrialization as a Historical Phenomenon, in R. Socolow, C. Andrews, F. Berkhout, and V. Thomas (eds.), *Industrial Ecology and Global Change*, Cambridge University Press, Cambridge.

Gupta, J. (1997). *The Climate Change Convention and Developing Countries: From Conflict to Consensus?*, Environment and Policy Series, Kluwer Academic Publishers, Dordrecht.

Gupta, J. (2000a). *Climate Change: Regime Development and Treaty Implementation in the Context of Unequal Power Relations*, Vol. 1, Institute for Environmental Studies, Vrije Universiteit, Amsterdam.

Gupta, J. (2000b). *On Behalf of My Delegation: A Guide for Developing Country Climate Negotiators*, Center for Sustainable Development of the Americas, Washington DC.

Gupta, J. and M. Grubb (eds.) (2000). *Climate Change and European Leadership: A Sustainable Role for Europe*, Environment and Policy Series, Kluwer Academic Publishers, Dordrecht.

Gupta, J., S. Maya, O. Kuik and A.N. Churie (1996). A Digest of Regional JI Issues: Overview of Results from National Consultations on Africa and JI, in R.S. Maya and J. Gupta (eds.) *Joint Implementation: Carbon Colonies or Business Opportunities? Weighing the Odds in an Information Vacuum*, Southern Centre, Zimbabwe, pp. 43–61.

Gupta, J. and L. Ringius (2001). The EU's Climate Leadership: Between Ambition and Reality, *International Environmental Agreements: Politics, Law and Economics*, Vol. 1, No. 2, pp. 281–99.

Gupta, J., P. van der Werff and F.G. Lebrun (2001a). *Bridging Interest, Classification and Technology Gaps in the Climate Change Regime*, Institute for Environmental Studies, Vrije Universiteit, Amsterdam.

Gupta, J., J. Vlasblom and C. Kroeze with contributions from C. Boudri and K. Dorland (2001b). *An Asian Dilemma: Modernising the Electricity Sector in China and India in the Context of Rapid Economic Growth and the Concern for Climate Change*, Institute for Environmental Studies, Report Number E-01/04, Amsterdam.

Hardin, G. (1968). The Tragedy of the Commons, *Science* 162, pp. 1243–8.

Hardin, G. (1974). Life-boat Ethics: The Case Against Helping the Poor, *Psychology Today*, Vol. 38–40, No. 41, September, p. 126.

Houghton, J.T., G.J. Jenkins and J.J. Ephraums (1990). *Climate Change: The IPCC Scientific Assessment*, Cambridge University Press, Cambridge.

Houghton, J.T., L.G. Meira Filho, J. Bruce, H. Lee, B.A. Callander, E. Haites, N. Harris and K. Maskell (eds.) (1995). *Climate Change 1994: Radiative Forcing of Climate Change and An Evaluation of the IPCC IS92 Emission Scenarios*, Cambridge University Press, Cambridge.

IPCC-I (2001). *Summary for Policymakers: A Report of Working Group I of the Intergovernmental Panel on Climate Change*, Cambridge University Press, Cambridge.

IPCC-II (2001). *Climate Change 2001: Impacts, Adaptation, and Vulnerability*, Cambridge University Press, Cambridge.

IPCC-III (2001). *Summary for Policymakers: A Report of Working Group III of the Intergovernmental Panel on Climate Change*, Cambridge University Press, Cambridge.

Jacobson H.K. and E.B. Weiss (1995). Strengthening Compliance with International Environmental Accords: Preliminary Observations from a Collaborative Project, in *Global Governance*, Vol. 1, No. 2, May–August, pp. 119–48.

Jansen, D. (1999). The Climate System, in P. Martens and J. Rotmans (eds.) *Climate Change: An Integrated Perspective*, Kluwer Academic Publishers, Dordrecht, pp. 11–50.

JIQ (2001). Advertisement by NIBO, *Joint Implementation Quarterly*, Vol. 7, No. 1, April, p. 3.

Jung, W. and R. Loske (2000). Issue Linkages to the Sustainability Agenda, in J. Gupta and M. Grubb (eds.) (2000). *Climate Change and European Leadership: A Sustainable Role for Europe*, Environment and Policy Series, Kluwer Academic Publishers, Dordrecht, pp. 157–72.

Kandlikar, M. and A. Sagar (1999). Climate Change Research and Analysis in India: An Integrated Assessment of a North–South Divide, *Global Environmental Change*, Vol. 9, pp. 119–38.

Khor, M. (2001). *Rethinking Globalization: Critical Issues and Policy Choices*, Zed Books, London.

Kim, J.-I. and L.J. Lau (1994). The Sources of Economic Growth of the East Asian Newly Industrialized Countries, *Journal of the Japanese and International Economies*, Vol. 8, pp. 235–71.

Kluger, J. and M.D. Lemonick (2001). A Climate of Despair, *Time Magazine*, 23 April, pp. 50–59.

Kothari, R. (1993). Towards a Politics of the South, in South Centre (ed.) *Facing the Challenge: Responses to the Report of the South Commission*, Zed Books, London, pp. 84–91.

Madeley, J. (2000). *Hungry for Trade: How the Poor Pay for Free Trade*, Zed Books, London.

Maurer, C. (2000). Rich Nations' Investments Heighten Climate Risk, *International Herald Tribune*, 18–19 November 2000, p. 14.

Maya, S. and J. Gupta (ed.) (1996). *Joint Implementation for Africa: Carbon Colonies or Business Opportunity? Weighing the Odds in an Information Vacuum*, Southern Centre, Zimbabwe.

McCormick, John (1999). The Role of Environmental NGOs in International Regimes, in N.J. Vig and R.S. Axelrod (eds.), *The Global Environment: Institutions, Law and Policy*, Earthscan, London, pp. 52–71.

McCormick, R.D. (2000). Charting a New Course for the Environment, *International Herald Tribune*, November 18–19, 2000, p. 14.

Meyer, A. (2000). *Contraction and Convergence: The Global Solution to Climate Change*, Schumacher Briefings, No. 5, Green Books for the Schumacher Society, Foxhole, Dartington, Totnes.

Mokyr, J. (1992). Institutions, Technological Creativity and Economic History, in A. Quadrio Curzio, M. Fortis and R. Zoboli (eds.) *Innovation, Resources and Economic Growth*, Springer Verlag, Berlin.

Moorcroft, D. (2000). From Anxiety to Action, *International Herald Tribune*, 18–19 November, p. 14.

Morgan, J. (2000). Loopholes in Treaty Could Harm the Environment, *International Herald Tribune*, 18–19 November, p. 13.

Mwandosya, M.J. (1999). *Survival Emissions: A Perspective from the South on Global Climate Change Negotiation*, DUP Ltd and The Centre for Energy, Environment, Science and Technology, Tanzania.

Nakićenović, N. *et al.* (2000). *Emissions Scenarios*, Cambridge University Press, Cambridge.

Nath, K. (1993). Selected Statements on Environment and Sustainable Development, Government of India.

Noordwijk Declaration on Climate Change (1989) in P. Vellinga, P. Kendall, and J. Gupta (eds.) *Noordwijk Conference Report*, Volume I, Ministry of Housing, Physical Planning and Environment, Netherlands.

Note by Secretariat to the AGBM (1997). Implementation of the Berlin Mandate: Additional Proposals from Parties. Addendum, Seventh Session, Bonn 31 July–7 August 1997, item 3 of the Provisional Agenda, FCCC/AGBM/1997/MISC.1/Add.3, pp. 20–21; cited also in CSE Dossier (1998) Factsheet 5, Centre for Science and Environment, New Delhi.

Nyerere, J. *et al.* (1990). *The Challenge to the South: The Report of the South Commission*, Oxford University Press, Oxford.

Oberthür, S. and H.E. Ott (1999). *The Kyoto Protocol: International Climate Policy for the 21st Century*, Springer Verlag, Berlin.

Ott, H. E. (2001). Climate Change: An Important Foreign Policy Issue, *International Affairs*, Vol. 77, No. 2, pp. 277–96.

Pearce, D.W. and C.A. Perrings (1995). Biodiversity Conservation and Economic Development: Local and Global Dimensions, in C.A. Perrings, K.-G.Mäler, C. Folke, C.S. Holling and B.-O. Jansson (eds.) *Biodiversity Conservation*, Kluwer Academic Publishers, Dordrecht, pp. 23–44.

Pearce, D., W.R. Cline, A.N. Achanta, S. Fankhauser, R.K. Pachauri, R.S.J. Tol and P. Vellinga (1995). The Social Costs of Climate Change, in J. Bruce, Hoesung Lee and E. Haites (eds.) *Climate Change 1995: Economic and Social Dimensions of Climate Change; Contribution of Working Group III to the Second Assessment Report of the Intergovernmental Panel on Climate Change*, Cambridge University Press, Cambridge, pp. 178–224.

Petrella, R. (2001). *The Water Manifesto: Arguments for a World Water Contract*, Zed Books, London.

Pew Centre/IHT (2000). Working Together for Success: Business Leaders Speak Out, Advertisement in *International Herald Tribune*, November 18–19, 2000, p. 16.

Pfaff, W. (2001). Kolonialisme Toen, Mondialisering Nu, *De Volkskrant*, 28 July, p. 7.

Phylipsen, G.J.M., J.W. Bode, K. Blok, H. Merkus, and B. Metz (1998). A Triptych Sectoral Approach to Burden Differentiation; GHG Emissions in the European Bubble, *Energy Policy*, Vol. 26, No. 12, pp. 929–43.

Prasad, M. (1990). Speech, in P. Vellinga, P. Kendall, J. Gupta, *et al.*, *Noordwijk Conference Report*, Volume I and II, Ministry of Housing, Physical Planning and Environment, Netherlands.

Prescott, J. (2000). It's Time For a Deal, *International Herald Tribune*, 18–19 November, p. 13.

Priem, H.N.A. (1995). De CO_2 Ideologie, Wetenschap en Onderwijs, NRC Handelsblad, 6 July, pp. 1–2.

Pritchett, Lant (1996). Forget Convergence: Divergence Past, Present and Future, *Finance and Development*, June, pp. 40–43.

Rao, P.V. Narasimha (1992). *Protecting the Environment: A Global Responsibility*,

Speech at Rio de Janeiro, Government of India, Ministry of Information and Broadcasting, No. 1/8/92.

Rao, P.V. Narasimha (1993). *Selected Speeches*, Vol. I, Government of India Publications Division.

Rao, P.V. Narasimha (1994). *Selected Speeches*, Vol.II, Government of India Publications Division.

Reilly, W. (1989). Statement of the United States of America, in P.Velling, P. Kendall, and J. Gupta (eds.) *Noordwijk Conference Report*, Volume II, Ministry of Housing, Physical Planning and Environment, Netherlands, pp. 115–18.

Roberts, A. and B. Kingsbury (1993). Introduction: The UN's Roles in International Society since 1945, in A. Roberts and B. Kingsbury (eds.) *United Nations, Divided World: The UN in International Relations*, Clarendon Press, Oxford, pp. 1–63.

Sachs, W., R. Loske, M. Linz et al. (1998). *Greening the North: A Post-Industrial Blueprint for Ecology and Equity*, Zed Books, London.

Sagar, A. and M. Kandlikar (1997). Knowledge, Rhetoric and Power: International Politics of Climate Change, *Economic and Political Weekly*, 6 December.

Salah, Ahmed Ben (1993). The South and the North: Neither Dictatorships nor Interference, in South Centre (ed.) *Facing the Challenge: Responses to the Report of the South Commission*, Zed Books, London, pp. 53–65.

Schelling, T.C. (1997). The Cost of Combating Global Warming: Facing the Trade-Offs, *Foreign Affairs*, Vol. 76, No. 6, pp. 8–14.

Schrijver, N. (1995). Sovereignty over Natural Resources: Balancing Rights and Duties in an Interdependent World, thesis, Rijksuniversiteit Groningen.

Sharma, V. (2001). Utilitarian Rationalism on Thin Ice, *Economic Times*, India, 6 January.

Slade, T.N. (1998). National Perspectives – Ratification and Implementation Strategies: The View from The Small Island States, paper presented at the conference: Climate After Kyoto – Implications for Energy, at Chatham House, 5–6 February.

South Centre (1993). An Overview and Summary of the Report of the South Commission, in South Centre (ed.) *Facing the Challenge: Responses to the Report of the South Commission*, Zed Books, London, pp. 3–52.

Stone, P.H. (1997). The Heat's On, *The National Journal*, Vol. 29–30, p. 1505.

SWCC (1990). Ministerial Declaration of the Second World Climate Conference and Scientific Declaration of the Second World Climate Conference, Geneva.

UNDP (1996). *Human Development Report 1996*, Oxford University Press, Oxford.

UNEP (2000). *Global Environmental Outlook*, Earthscan, London.

Van de Woerd, K.F., C.M. de Wit, A. Kolk, D.L. Levy, P. Vellinga and E. Behlyarova (2000). *Diverging Business Strategies Towards Climate Change*, Institute for Environmental Studies, Vrije Universiteit, Amsterdam.

Venugopalachari, S. (1997). Inaugural Address, on the Occasion of the

Conference on Activities Implemented Jointly, New Delhi, 8 January.

Victor, D. and J.E. Salt (1995). Keeping the Climate Treaty Relevant, commentary in *Nature*, Vol. 373, 26 January.

Wallace, D. (1996). *Sustainable Industrialisation*, Royal Institute of International Affairs/Earthscan, London.

Watson, R.T., I.R. Noble, B. Bolin, N.H. Ravindranath, D.J. Verardo and D.J. Dokken (2000). *Land Use, Land-Use Change, and Forestry*, IPCC, Cambridge University Press, Cambridge.

Watson, R.T., M.C. Zinoera, R.H. Moss, and D.J. Dokken (1998). *The Regional Impacts of Climate Change: An Assessment of Vulnerability*, Cambridge University Press, Cambridge.

Weiszäcker, E.von, (1999). Dematerialisation, in P. Vellinga, F. Berkhout and J. Gupta (eds.) *Managing a Material World: Reflections on Industrial Ecology*, Environment and Policy Series, Kluwer Academic Publishers, Dordrecht.

Weiszäcker, E.von, A. Lovins and H. Lovins (1997). *Factor Four, Doubling Wealth and Halving Resource Use*, Earthscan, London.

Wettestad, J. (2000) The Complicated Development of EU Climate Policy, in J. Gupta and M. Grubb (eds.) *Climate Change and European Leadership: A Sustainable Role for Europe*, Environment and Policy Series, Kluwer Academic Publishers, Dordrecht.

Wolters, G., J. Swager and J. Gupta (1991). Climate Change: A Brief History of Global, Regional and National Policy Measures, Paper of the Dutch Ministry of Housing, Physical Planning and Environment presented at the International Global Warming Symposium, organised by the Japan Society for Air Pollution, 15 November.

Womack, J.P., D.T. Jones and D. Roos (1990). *The Machine that Changed the World*, Rawson Associates, New York.

WRI (1994). *World Resources 1994–1995*, World Resources Institute, Washington DC, pp. 362–4.

WWF (2000). *Make-or-Break the Kyoto Protocol,* Worldwide Fund for Nature International.

Yamin, F. (1998). The Kyoto Protocol: Origins, Assessment and Future Challenges, *Review of European Community and International Environmental Law*, Vol. 7, No. 2, pp. 113–27.

Yamin, F. (2000). The Role of the EU in Climate Negotiations, in J. Gupta and M. Grubb (eds.) *Climate Change and European Leadership: A Sustainable Role for Europe*, Environment and Policy Series, Kluwer Academic Publishers, Dordrecht, pp. 47–66.

Young Oran, R. and Konrad von Moltke (1994). The Consequences of International Environmental Regimes, Report from the Barcelona Workshop. *International Environmental Affairs*, 6, pp. 348–70.

Zhang, Z.X. (1999). Is China Taking Action to Limit its Greenhouse Gas Emissions? Past Evidence and Future Prospects, in J. Goldemberg and W. Reid (eds.) *Promoting Development While Limiting Greenhouse Gas Emissions: Trends and Baselines*, UNDP and WRI, New York.

APPENDIX

USEFUL ORGANISATIONS AND WEBSITES

IPCC Secretariat in Geneva: email ipcc_sec@gateway.wmo.ch.

GLOSSARIES

Glossary of Climate Change Acronyms and Jargon, United Nations – Framework Convention on Climate Change: http://www.unfccc.int/siteinfo/glossary.html

Glossary of Climate Change Terms, United States Environmental Protection Agency, Global Warming Site: http://www.epa.gov/globalwarming/glossary.html

COUNTRY POSITIONS ON CLIMATE CHANGE

AOSIS (climate change position not described): http://www.sidsnet.org
Canada: http://www.climatechange.gc.ca/
EU: http://europa.eu.int/geninfo/query_fr.htm and http://europa.eu.int/
G77 (climate change position not described): http://www.g-77.org
OECD (general information about climate change): http://www.oecd.org/env/cc/index.htm; 'OECD Perspectives on Climate Change Policies' (1999), http://www.oecd.org/env/docs/cc/cop5-statement.pdf
OPEC (climate change position not described): http://www.opec.org/
US: http://www.epa.gov/globalwarming/index.html

NGO, BUSINESS AND SCIENTIFIC WEBSITES

Climate Action Network: http://www.igc.org/climate/eco.html
Business for Social Responsibility: http://www.bsr.org
Coalition for Environmentally Responsible Economies: http://www.ceres.org
Consumer's Choice Council: http://www.consumerscouncil.org
Global Climate Coalition: http://www.globalclimate.org
Intergovernmental Panel on Climate Change: http://www.ipcc.ch

Pew Center: http://www.pewclimate.org/projects/index.html
International Institute for Sustainable Development: http://iisd.ca/ic/
World Business Council for Sustainable Development: http://www.wbcsd.ch/
  websearc.htm; http://www.wbcsd.org
World Resources Institute: http://www.wri.org
Worldwide Fund for Nature: http://www.wwf.org

INDEX

THE GLOBAL ISSUES SERIES

Already available

Robert Ali Brac de la Perrière and Franck Seuret, *Brave New Seeds: The Threat of GM Crops to Farmers*

Oswaldo de Rivero, *The Myth of Development: The Non-viable Economies of the 21st Century*

Joyeeta Gupta, *Our Simmering Planet: What to do about Global Warming?*

Nicholas Guyatt, *Another American Century? The United States and the World after 2000*

Martin Khor, *Rethinking Globalization: Critical Issues and Policy Choices*

John Madeley, *Hungry for Trade: How the Poor Pay for Free Trade*

Riccardo Petrella, *The Water Manifesto: Arguments for a World Water Contract*

Vandana Shiva, *Protect or Plunder? Understanding Intellectual Property Rights*

Harry Shutt, *A New Democracy: Alternatives to a Bankrupt World Order*

In preparation

Peggy Antrobus and Gigi Francisco, *The Women's Movement Worldwide: Issues and Strategies for the New Century*

Amit Bhaduri and Deepak Nayyar, *Free Market Economics: The Intelligent Person's Guide to Liberalization*

Jonathan Bloch and Paul Todd, *Business as Usual? Intelligence Agencies and Secret Services in the New Century*

Julian Burger, *First Peoples: What Future?*

Richard Douthwaite, *Go for Growth? Poverty, the Environment and the Pros and Cons of Economic Growth*

Graham Dunkley, *Trading Development: Trade, Globalization and Alternative Development Possibilities*

John Howe, *A Ticket to Ride: Breaking the Transport Gridlock*

Calestous Juma, *The New Genetic Divide: Biotechnology in the Age of Globalization*

John Madeley, *Food for All: The Need for a New Agriculture*

Jeremy Seabrook, *The Future of Culture: Can Human Diversity Survive in a Globalized World?*

David Sogge, *Give and Take: What's the Matter with Foreign Aid?*

Keith Suter, *Curbing Corporate Power: How Can We Control Transnational Corporations?*

Oscar Ugarteche, *A Level Playing Field: Changing the Rules of the Global Economy*

Nedd Willard, *The Drugs War: Is This the Solution?*

For full details of this list and Zed's other subject and general catalogues, please write to: The Marketing Department, Zed Books, 7 Cynthia Street, London NI 9JF, UK or email Sales@zedbooks. demon.co.uk
Visit our website at: www.zedbooks.demon.co.uk

Participating Organizations

Both ENDS   A service and advocacy organization which collaborates with environment and indigenous organizations, both in the South and in the North, with the aim of helping to create and sustain a vigilant and effective environmental movement.

> Damrak 28-30, 1012 LJ Amsterdam, The Netherlands
> Phone: +31 20 623 0823   Fax: +31 20 620 8049
> Email: info@bothends.org
> Website: www.bothends.org

Catholic Institute for International Relations (CIIR)   CIIR aims to contribute to the eradication of poverty through a programme that combines advocacy at national and international level with community-based development.

> Unit 3, Canonbury Yard, 190a New North Road, London N1 7BJ, UK
> Phone +44 (0)20 7354 0883   Fax +44 (0)20 7359 0017
> Email: ciir@ciir.org
> Website: www.ciir.org

Corner House   The Corner House is a UK-based research and solidarity group working on social and environmental justice issues in North and South.

> PO Box 3137, Station Road, Sturminster Newton, Dorset DT10 1YJ, UK
> Tel.: +44 (0)1258 473795   Fax: +44 (0)1258 473748
> Email: cornerhouse@gn.apc.org
> Website: www.cornerhouse.icaap.org

Council on International and Public Affairs (CIPA)   CIPA is a human rights research, education and advocacy group, with a particular focus on economic and social rights in the USA and elsewhere around the world. Emphasis in recent years has been given to resistance to corporate domination.

> 777 United Nations Plaza, Suite 3C, New York, NY 10017, USA
> Tel. +1 212 972 9877   Fax +1 212 972 9878
> E-mail: cipany@igc.org
> Website: www.cipa-apex.org

Dag Hammarskjöld Foundation   The Dag Hammarskjöld Foundation, established 1962, organises seminars and workshops on social, economic and cultural issues facing developing countries with a particular focus on alternative and innovative solutions. Results are published in its journal *Develpment Dialogue*.

Övre Slottsgatan 2, 753 10 Uppsala, Sweden.
Tel.: +46 18 102772   Fax: +46 18 122072
e-mail: secretariat@dhf.uu.se
Website: www.dhf.uu.se

Development GAP The Development Group for Alternative Policies is a Non-Profit Development Resource Organization working with popular organizations in the South and their Northern partners in support of a development that is truly sustainable and that advances social justice.

927 15th Street NW, 4th Floor, Washington, DC, 20005, USA
Tel.: +1 202 898 1566   Fax: +1 202 898 1612
E-mail: dgap@igc.org
Website: www.developmentgap.org

Focus on the Global South Focus is dedicated to regional and global policy analysis and advocacy work. It works to strengthen the capacity of organizations of the poor and marginalized people of the South and to better analyse and understand the impacts of the globalization process on their daily lives.

C/o CUSRI, Chulalongkorn University, Bangkok 10330, Thailand
Tel.: +66 2 218 7363 Fax: +66 2 255 9976
Email: Admin@focusweb.org
Website: www.focusweb.org

Inter Pares Inter Pares, a Canadian social justice organization, has been active since 1975 in building relationships with Third World development groups and providing support for community-based development programs. Inter Pares is also involved in education and advocacy in Canada, promoting understanding about the causes, effects and solutions to poverty.

58 rue Arthur Street, Ottawa, Ontario, KIR 7B9 Canada
Phone +1 613 563 4801   Fax +1 613 594 4704

Public Interest Research Centre PIRC is a research and campaigning group based in Delhi which seeks to serve the information needs of activists and organizations working on macro-economic issues concerning finance, trade and development.

142 Maitri Apartments, Plot No. 28, Patparganj, Delhi 110092, India
Phone: +91 11 2221081/2432054   Fax: +91 11 2224233
Email: kaval@nde.vsnl.net.in

Third World Network   TWN is an international network of groups and individuals involved in efforts to bring about a greater articulation of the needs and rights of peoples in the Third World; a fair distribution of the world's resources; and forms of development which are ecologically sustainable and fulfil human needs. Its international secretariat is based in Penang, Malaysia.

228 Macalister Road, 10400 Penang, Malaysia
Tel.: +60 4 226 6159   Fax: +60 4 226 4505
Email: twnet@po.jaring.my
Website: www.twnside.org.sg

Third World Network–Africa   TWN–Africa is engaged in research and advocacy on economic, environmental and gender issues. In relation to its current particular interest in globalization and Africa, its work focuses on trade and investment, the extractive sectors and gender and economic reform.

2 Ollenu Street, East Legon, PO Box AN19452, Accra-North, Ghana.
Tel.: +233 21 511189/503669/500419   Fax: +233 21 511188
email: twnafrica@ghana.com

World Development Movement (WDM)   The World Development Movement campaigns to tackle the causes of poverty and injustice. It is a democratic membership movement that works with partners in the South to cancel unpayable debt and break the ties of IMF conditionality, for fairer trade and investment rules, and for strong international rules on multinationals.

25 Beehive Place, London SW9 7QR, UK
Tel.: +44 (0)20 7737 6215   Fax: +44 (0)20 7274 8232
E-mail: wdm@wdm.org.uk
Website: www.wdm.org.uk

THIS BOOK IS ALSO AVAILABLE
IN THE FOLLOWING COUNTRIES

EGYPT

MERIC
(The Middle East Readers'
Information Center)
2 Bahgat Ali Street,
Tower D/Apt. 24
Zamalek
Cairo
Tel: 20 2 735 3818/736 3824
Fax: 20 2 736 9355

FIJI

University Book Centre,
University of South Pacific,
Suva
Tel: 679 313 900
Fax: 679 303 265

GHANA

EPP Book Services,
PO Box TF 490,
Trade Fair,
Accra
Tel: 233 21 778347
Fax: 233 21 779099

MOZAMBIQUE

Sul Sensações
PO Box 2242,
Maputo
Tel: 258 1 421974
Fax: 258 1 423414

NAMIBIA

Book Den
PO Box 3469
Shop 4, Frans Indongo Gardens
Windhoek
Tel: 264 61 239976
Fax: 264 61 234248

NEPAL

Everest Media Services,
GPO Box 5443, Dillibazar
Putalisadak Chowk

Kathmandu
Tel: 977 1 416026
Fax: 977 1 250176

PAPUA NEW GUINEA

Unisearch PNG Pty Ltd
Box 320, University
National Capital District
Tel: 675 326 0130
Fax: 675 326 0127

RWANDA

Librairie Ikirezi
PO Box 443
Kigali
Tel/Fax: 250 71314

SUDAN

The Nile Bookshop
New Extension Street 41
P O Box 8036
Khartoum
Tel: 249 11 463749

TANZANIA

TEMA Publishing Co Ltd
PO Box 63115
Dar Es Salaam
Tel: 255 22 2113608
Fax: 255 22 2110472

UGANDA

Aristoc Booklex Ltd
PO Box 5130, Kampala Road
Diamond Trust Building
Kampala
Tel: 256 41 344381/349052
Fax: 256 41 254867

ZAMBIA

UNZA Press
PO Box 32379
Lusaka
Tel: 260 1 290409
Fax: 260 1 253952